London Publishing Partnership — *A Better Politics*

DANNY DORLING is the Halford Mackinder Professor of Geography at the University of Oxford. He grew up in Oxford and went to university in Newcastle upon Tyne. He has worked in Newcastle, Bristol, Leeds, Sheffield and New Zealand. With a group of colleagues he helped create the website www.worldmapper.org, which shows who has most and least in the world. Much of Danny's work is available open access (see www.dannydorling.org). His work concerns issues of housing, health, employment, education and poverty.

His many books (some co-authored) include *Injustice: Why Social Inequality Still Persists* (Policy Press, 2015), *Inequality and the 1%* (Verso, 2014), *The Social Atlas of Europe* (with D. Ballas and B. D. Hennig; Policy Press, 2014), *All That Is Solid: The Great Housing Disaster* (Allen Lane, 2015), *Population 10 Billion* (Constable, 2013), *So You Think You Know About Britain?* (Constable, 2011), *The Visualization of Social Spatial Structure* (Wiley, 2012), *Geography* (with C. Lee; Profile, 2016) and *People and Places: A 21st-Century Atlas of the UK* (with B. Thomas; Policy Press, 2016).

T0159569

A Better Politics

PERSPECTIVES

Series editor: Diane Coyle

A Better Politics

How Government Can Make Us Happier

Danny Dorling

with illustrations
by Ella Furness

LONDON PUBLISHING PARTNERSHIP

Published by London Publishing Partnership
www.londonpublishingpartnership.co.uk

Published in association with
Enlightenment Economics
www.enlightenmenteconomics.com

ISBN: 978-1-907994-53-1 (pbk)

A catalogue record for this book is
available from the British Library

This book has been composed in Candara

Copy-edited and typeset by
T&T Productions Ltd, London
www.tandtproductions.com

Printed by Page Bros, Norwich

To Dimitris Ballas

Maslow's 'hierarchy of needs',
as interpreted by Ella Furness

Happiness is about the heartland[1]

Contents

Foreword

This book is grounded in an understanding of what drives real people and what really matters in life. For those who accepted the narrative of austerity but are now wondering why it doesn't feel right, this book is a must-read.

The thing that's lacking in the often machine-like short-term tactics of British politics is any vision of what we could be as individuals and as a nation. Danny Dorling makes simple arguments for a better society – ideas that are grounded in practical idealism and backed up with intelligent interpretation of evidence and data. In Britain today there is little counter-narrative to the 'me first', humans-as-commodity culture we appear to be sliding inexorably towards. Here, fairness isn't used as a tool to judge politics or policymakers – and it is determined by those with power, as opposed to those without.

Dorling's book gives examples of the development of alternative views of commerce and relationships – ideas that are gaining credibility in spite of the prevailing discourse, and which could change this country, and possibly the world, for the better.

The future is often decided by the things we fail to debate. This book is a call to discuss things that have become uncomfortable for politicians; it's a call to the future of policymaking and to the role of government in creating the conditions for human policy. We need to listen carefully.

Lord Victor O. Adebowale CBE, *Crossbench Peer*

Preface

The aim of this book is to inspire a better politics: one that will enable future generations to be happier. While its publication coincides with the 500th anniversary of Thomas More's *Utopia*, its proposals are not a utopian wish-list. They are, crucially, a set of policy suggestions that are already in place (or are being tested) elsewhere in Europe; proposals that address the issues that appear to matter most to people in the UK.

In the immediate aftermath of a global financial crash it is hard to imagine great progress, as it also was after the crash of 1929. What I suggest here is in many ways much less imaginative than setting up a National Health Service would have sounded in 1935, or the suggestion also made at that time that full employment was possible in the near future – but both of those things happened.

Most of the policy proposals I put forward are not fully polished. Some might turn out to be unworkable, while others may not seem bold enough with the benefit of hindsight. None of us can know for sure what proportion of what we suggest will turn out to be misguided, or where we might have hit the nail on the head. That is often only apparent in retrospect.

What is certain is that there is no shortage of evidence, ideas and choices for us to consider if we wish to. There are many policies that we could adopt if we really want to be collectively happier and healthier. We *could* have a government that makes our lives happier, if we win the argument for it.

Acknowledgements

I am very grateful to the following for various comments on various stages of the manuscript that became this book: Richard Baggaley, Dimitris Ballas, Florence Rose Burton, Sarah Campbell, Sam Clark, Diane Coyle, David Dorling, Dawn Foster, Amanda Goodall, Aniko Horvath, Vittal Katikireddi, Carl Lee, Chris Lynch, Avril Maddrell, Connor McCarthy, Paul Nicolson, Andrew Oswald, Karen Shook, Natasha Stotesbury, Sally Tomlinson, Kathy Wrigley and Terry Wrigley. Many thanks are also due to Ailsa Allen for drawing all the graphs and tables.

Danny Dorling, *University of Oxford**

---

* Oxford: 'that crowded, clucking duckpond of vanity and ruffled feathers'.[2]

Chapter 1

Introduction

> To make a real difference we need to shift common
> sense, change the terms of debate and shape a new
> political terrain.
> — *Doreen Massey*[3]

The aim of this book is to inspire a better politics:
one that will enable future generations to be happier, with goals of greater well-being and better health,
rather than wealth maximization. Happiness does not
mean being ecstatic: it is the avoidance of misery, the
gaining of long-term life satisfaction, the feeling of ful-
filment, of worth, of kindness, of usefulness and of love.
We need new measures of what matters most to us.

The book is also about 'the collective good'. We cannot truly be happy if those around us are not happy.
Not just our family and friends, but our fellow citizens,
whose lives are entwined with ours and will affect us
for good or ill at some point. This book looks at evidence and suggests policies that take account of that
evidence. We live in an information-rich, 'scientific'

world, but this is a recent phenomenon. Yet while we might not fully understand climate change or sub-atomic physics, we should now find it easier to understand what makes us happy; and we can also compare ourselves with other nations on key measures of health and well-being.

Politicians often say that they are addressing the issues that matter most to people. But they rely on opinion surveys in which the questions have been predetermined. What have people themselves said, unprompted, about what is most important to them or their family? How do their answers relate to how happy and healthy those same people are?

Being happy is not the be-all and end-all, but it's better to be happier if you can. Politicians often promise that if they are elected they will ensure that the electorate will be 'better off' than if the other lot are elected; but do politicians actually know what it is that makes people happy? Other academics have approached this question in many very different ways.[4]

This book begins with statistical evidence from a scientific paper. Yet although almost all of the facts presented in these pages are referenced, it is not a research-based volume. Instead, this book is a collection of ideas – based mostly on the work of others, including much readily available evidence – on what policies could best safeguard us (better than current policies) from what the evidence indicates harms us the most.

Before going any further, why might you want to consider the arguments and evidence presented in this book? One reason is that, while it isn't exactly a new phenomenon, inequality in our society is getting worse – particularly when we look at the growing gap between the very wealthy and the rest, including those with least. This matters because it appears that growing inequality can make it harder to enact the policies that could most improve our happiness.

When it was first observed that despite rising average material wealth, people were not happier than their parents had been, researchers in economics – not in psychology, sociology or politics – began to ask why. Recently, many economists have pointed out that old economic growth models, those used by both the left and the right, were failing.[5] The new models concern findings that could not have been made a generation ago, because then it was true that well-being was generally increased by having more material goods. A generation ago, what people needed above all else was a good enough home to live in and the means to be able to keep it warm. A generation or so before that, most people in the UK did not have spare clothes, or enough money to eat well most of the time. In our generation, many of us eat too much. Most people, although far from all, now have enough.

Recent research has shown that now, living in a country with higher levels of well-organized collective spending produces a happier population; and that when countries are compared, public policies such as social insurance and employment protection are among the most important factors in predicting well-being among citizens. This may come as a surprise if you think that being taxed as little as possible is what gives people the most economic freedom and leads to them enjoying 'life, liberty and the pursuit of happiness' to the fullest. It is worth reflecting that Thomas Jefferson wrote those famous words into the American Constitution. Many believe that he took inspiration for this from John Locke, who had written, in his 'Essay concerning human understanding', that 'The highest perfection of intellectual nature lies in a careful and constant pursuit of true and solid happiness.'

Economist Benjamin Radcliff summarized his research findings on this for an American audience:

> The differences in your feeling of well-being living in a Scandinavian country (where welfare programs are large) versus the US are going to be larger than the individual factors in your life. The political differences trump all the individual things you're supposed to do to make yourself happier – to have fulfilling personal relationships, to have a job, to have more income. The political factors swamp all those individual factors. Countries with high levels of gross domestic product consumed by government have higher levels of personal satisfaction.[6]

Radcliff is correct about the correlations when happiness is measured carefully,[7] but of course people do not wake up each day and check how much their government spends and feel happier if taxation and public spending is higher. Living in better-organized (and often higher-taxing) countries makes leading our personal lives easier, allows us to get on with our families, and with other people more widely. (Although there are also societies where overall taxation is lower but where income inequality is lower and well-being is higher than in the UK.[8])

Until recently, economists' models have maximized what they call 'utility': the satisfaction achieved from the consumption of a good or service given individual preferences. However, a growing number of economists have, in the last twenty years, started looking at happiness instead.[9] Before the 2008 crash, some leading economists began arguing that there were things that were much more important to life and well-being than money. For example, Ann Pettifor[10] and Anastasia Nesvetailova[11] foresaw the turmoil to come in 2008 and argued that there was a need for new understanding in economics. That new understanding should include a better appreciation of happiness.

Alois Stutzer and Bruno Frey have recently shown that people in more consumerist societies are likely to overestimate how much enjoyment they will gain from the goods they consume, and they discount the harm working too many hours and commuting too much will cause them. As Stutzer and Frey put it, 'suboptimal choices result'.[12] Even more recently, John Helliwell has shown that environmental sustainability depends on well-being:

> If people really are happier working together for a worthy purpose, this exposes a multitude of win–win solutions to material problems, thereby building community while meeting material needs.[13]

This new thinking has wide-reaching implications. It has emerged because we are so much better off, in material ways, than our parents were – and yet no happier.

As happiness economics is based on relating well-being to other life events, economists Gus O'Donnell and Andrew Oswald have recently explained that the new economic research has:

> one strength that may not be completely recognized by all economists. People are not asked how much one thing makes them happy compared to another. Deeply complicated cause-and-effect survey questions are thereby largely eschewed, and that is an advantage.[14]

You do not ask people what they think makes them happy, but instead observe how their levels of happiness change and try to associate that with other changes in their lives at that time.

This book is heavily influenced by happiness economics, but I am not an economist and so it also uses a wider range of sources from the social sciences, humanities and sciences, and includes many examples from current affairs. To present consistent evidence, results from a single survey of happiness are referred to, but it is important to recognize the much wider context to this work. Many recent studies point in similar directions. The sense that it is time we measured success differently is infectious. On 28 June 2012, the General Assembly of the United Nations agreed to pass resolution A/RES/66/281, which states that:

> The General Assembly, ... Conscious that the pursuit of happiness is a fundamental human goal, ... Recognizing also the need for a more inclusive, equitable and balanced approach to economic growth that promotes sustainable development, poverty eradication, happiness and the well-being of all peoples, decides to proclaim 20 March the International Day of Happiness.[15]

Thomas Jefferson might have approved.

So what does promote happiness? To try to answer this question, in 2006 a colleague and I investigated some data about what is most important to people, and how that might relate to their health and happiness. More recent work by others suggests that what we found a decade ago continues to hold true.[16] In Britain, a large household panel study has been conducted annually for the past twenty-five years. In four of those years (September 1992 to December 1995) an unusual question was added. It was unusual because to answer this question, you had to write in an answer. Here is the question. Try it yourself in relation to the most recent twelve months:

> *State in your own words what in the last year has happened to you (or your family) which stood out as important.*

It is a straightforward question. So please record your responses, but don't feel bad if you don't have four.

> *Up to four responses can be recorded.*
>
> 1. ....
>
> 2. ....
>
> 3. ....
>
> 4. ....

Over ten years later I remain shocked by the responses people gave. It is fair to say that this question was asked at the end of a very long interview-style survey. Perhaps many people were simply sick of answering questions. Maybe they thought that some of the answers they had already given covered everything that mattered. Nevertheless, a large and representative sample of the population answered, so it is worth considering carefully what they said.

In the UK, in those years (1992–1995), a majority of the up-to-four answers were left blank: 'Nothing else of importance happened to us'. Most people only noted down one or two things. There were as many people recording nothing at all as there were people who listed three or four events.

Nothing happens to most people most of the time; at least nothing that they would say is important to them. Out of the 143,860[17] possible opportunities to give responses to that question in this survey over those years, 94,911 (66%) were either left blank or filled in as something equivalent to 'nothing'. The second most common response was to state that someone in your *family* other than you had ended or started a relationship (3,728 events, 3%). The third most common was to report that *you* had gone on holiday (3,635, 3% again), the fourth most common was that *you* had moved home (2,810, 2%), and the fifth most common was that something had happened to *your* health (2,678 responses, 2%). Many more than 2% of people move home in a given year, but for many who do it was just not an important enough event to list.

People are very forgetful. Men are more likely to be forgetful than women.[18] The survey revealed that men who have just become fathers are far less likely to list their new baby as an important event than women who have just become mothers. One of the first things we discover is that life is *not that eventful* for many people much of the time, but also that the usual preoccupations of the media tend not to appear. When unprompted, hardly anyone answers 'immigration to Britain rose and this harmed me and my family' or 'I worried about government economic policy this year'. Respondents also do not mention terrorism, or at least they did not at the time of those surveys.[19]

So, if you struggled to come up with four important things that happened to you or your family in the past twelve months, don't despair, but please do write in an answer on at least one of the four lines above if you can – and then I'll ask you one more question at the start of the next chapter.

As I'll explain below, it turns out that half of all the important things that happened to people in the past year were not associated with being significantly happier. For example, most health-related events were not, on average, good news for most people. You probably do not want any of the four most important things that happened to you in the last year to concern your health. Worry, anxiety and clinically diagnosed depression are now rising generation after generation among young people in the most unequal of affluent countries.[20] This affects the children of the rich in our society just as much as those of affluent, average, modest or poor backgrounds.

A better politics is not simply a politics that maximizes individual happiness related to everyday events, including those important, personal events. We also gain happiness from clean air and green spaces in ways that surveys (such as the one used here) cannot pick up, even though other studies do.[21] Governments also need to consider long-term issues such as climate change, species extinction, pollution and avoiding war, famine and plagues.[22] But governments – the politicians that constitute them, the civil servants who work for them, and all of us who vote – also occasionally need to be reminded of what it is that actually preoccupies most people.

The UK prime minister at the time of writing, David Cameron, floated the idea of the government monitoring happiness in 2005, and introduced a happiness index in 2010.[23] In 2015 the first baseline measures were published.[24] It will be interesting to see how they have changed by 2020. A recent report sponsored by the UK government described 'the most compelling evidence' for a link between economic performance and higher well-being. This came from a study of a manufacturing plant in Finland, which found that a one-point increase in job satisfaction (on a six-point scale) resulted in a 9% increase in productivity.[25]

My first and most important suggestion for a better politics is that governments should concern themselves with what matters most to people, according to the evidence. This means people have to be asked.

The next chapter explores what we can learn from surveys that do just that. The results are surprising. They hold valuable lessons for politicians, no matter what party they represent.

Chapter 2

Basic needs

Human beings, who are almost unique in having the
ability to learn from the experience of others, are also
remarkable for their apparent disinclination to do so.
— *Douglas Adams and Mark Carwardine*[26]

It was ten years ago, just before the global financial
crisis, that my colleague Dimitris Ballas and I conducted
our experiment using the answers people had written at
the end of the survey described above. We tried to discover the secret to happiness. We coupled the answers
with additional data on the same people's state of happiness. Events that in retrospect stood out as important to
you or your family are good potential candidates for the
things that significantly affected your state of happiness.

One reason to search for the secret to happiness was
that many researchers had begun to worry that something was wrong. My colleague Dimitris is an economist
by background, and had been trained to consider people
as rational economic agents, all continually aiming to
maximize their individual satisfaction or 'utility'.[27] In the

orthodox theory, wider society was of little importance. But what if many people individually striving to maximize their own utility cause harm, in aggregate, to the crowd? And what if one needs to be part of a happy crowd to maximize one's own happiness?

So now here's the second question.

> *Have you recently been feeling reasonably happy, all things considered?*

Take your pick and please circle *just one* answer below: 1, 2 or 3.

> *1. No, I've generally felt less than reasonably happy.*
>
> *2. I've felt the same as usual.*
>
> *3. Actually, I've felt more than reasonably happy.*

If you answered 1 or 3, why? What has made you more or less happy? Do you know? Is it possible to know and articulate your feeling as a number? Might it be in your nature to be happier than might reasonably be expected, or less happy than you consider it would be reasonable to be?

Here, the baseline is the level of happiness it is reasonable to expect. It is admittedly vague and, by definition, highly subjective. Yet this was exactly how the question was put to participants in the British Household Panel Surveys of the 1990s.

Dimitris and I compared what unprompted events people recorded in the survey with their average reported levels of happiness, and we tabulated our findings. As this book is using our results, there is a large extract from that table below (see table 1). Lamentably, the table does not give the answer to life, the universe and everything, but it is an attempt to summarize what appears to matter most to the lives of typical British people in the 1990s.

What mattered most in the 1990s is probably still of most significance to people today. Furthermore, it takes many years to digest the results of data like this and to begin to link this table to other political, economic and social events and subsequent evidence. Also, later surveys tend not to ask people these questions so directly and without prompts.

It turns out that many of the answers that we found to be important have been known for a very long time. And, in hindsight, they are not that surprising. But it may also be the case that people can forget what matters most. The UK in the past forty years appears to have become one of those more forgetful places.

Another reason you haven't heard of our findings before is because the table was titled 'OLS regression equation of subjective happiness and major life events (adjusted for gender, age, age squared and education)'. Both that title and the fact that it was printed on page 1,249 of a very academic journal understandably helped put people off the scent.[28]

Now the time is right to reveal all.

The answer to the secret of happiness is … '34' – a little lower than the '42' prophesied by Douglas Adams in *The Hitchhiker's Guide to the Galaxy*.

There are thirty-four events that happen in our lives with sufficient frequency and importance to warrant consideration here. The most common is 'Nothing important happened to us this year'. If you replied earlier that you are a little less happy than usual, as nothing important has happened to you recently, then you are not alone. Everybody hurts (sometimes).

Table 1 lists the thirty-four 'things' that can happen to you in the order of those most likely to correlate with you reporting greater happiness to those most correlated with reporting the least happiness. In the second column of the table, the effect of each event is modified by how frequently it occurs, and the final column shows the ranking based on that prevalence. For any individual, it is the first and third columns of the table that matter most. We cannot be happy all the time, because many sad things will happen to us, but we can at least begin to concentrate more on what it is that matters most, and try a little harder to prevent or delay that which harms our happiness the most, rather than concentrating on trying to achieve things that are not so strongly associated with well-being.

This book is ordered into chapters that group the events listed below into a well-known hierarchy of

Table 1. OLS regression equation of subjective happiness and major life events (adjusted for gender, age, age squared and education). British Household Panel Survey waves 1992–95 (pooled and weighted on the basis of the 1995 cross-sectional weights; note that the value of the constant is 2.25).

Life event	Coefficient	Frequency (%) × regression coefficient	Original regression rank	Prevalence-based regression rank
Relationships (mine ending 36, 43)	−0.178	−0.08	1	6
Death (parent, 45)	−0.166	−0.08	2	5
Health parent (1–9)	−0.139	−0.06	3	7
Death (other 45)	−0.137	−0.04	4	11
Employment job loss (24)	−0.129	−0.12	5	3
Health mine (1–9)	−0.117	−0.22	6	2
Death (family 45)	−0.098	−0.11	7	4
Health partner (1–9)	−0.092	−0.05	8	9
Health child (1–9)	−0.084	−0.04	9	13
Health other (1–9)	−0.073	−0.05	10	8
Education child (12–19)	−0.029	−0.04	11	12
Employment other (23, 26–29)	−0.028	−0.04	12	15
Other event (10–11, 32–34, 37–39, 90–95)	−0.026	−0.04	13	10
Nothing important happened	−0.022	−1.47	14	1
Relationships (pet ownership/ companionship 54)	−0.020	−0.01	15	17
Finance (other 60–69, 73–79)	−0.019	−0.03	16	16
Relationships family (46–53, 55–59)	−0.014	−0.04	17	14
Relationships (family 35, 41–42)	0.002	0.91	18	18
Leisure (our holiday 30)	0.010	0.61	19	20
Moving home (44, 80–81)	0.013	0.46	20	24
Education other (12–19)	0.024	0.27	21	21
Finance (car 70)	0.027	0.02	22	22
Leisure (my holiday 30)	0.029	0.07	23	30
Pregnancy/birth (other 40)	0.031	0.00	24	19
Pregnancy/birth (family 40)	0.034	0.03	25	25
Relationships (child's starting 35, 42)	0.037	0.02	26	23
Employment job change (20–21)	0.040	0.07	27	29
Leisure (other 30–31)	0.043	0.05	28	28
Education mine (12–19)	0.052	0.08	29	33
Pregnancy/birth (child's 40)	0.053	0.05	30	26
Pregnancy/birth (mine 40)	0.084	0.08	31	31
Finance (house 71)	0.097	0.05	32	27
Employment job gain 22	0.097	0.08	33	32
Relationships (mine starting 35, 42)	0.160	0.18	34	34

Note: health-related events include 'negative' (e.g. injury) as well as 'positive' events (e.g. recovery, positive test results). The same applies to many of the other variables listed here. See the appendix for a detailed description of all subject codes and event category codes.

Source: table based on table 3 in Ballas and Dorling (2007) (see endnote 17).

Explanatory notes for table 1

Life event: the independent variables (like 'pregnancy/birth'). For a detailed description of these and their numbering, see the appendix.

Coefficient: an estimate of the amount by which the subjective level of happiness (the dependent variable) is affected by the independent variable in question, with the other independent variables held constant. Range: negative (decreases happiness) to positive (increases it). 0 = has no effect on happiness.

Frequency (%) × regression coefficient: adjustment to the coefficient based on the prevalence or likelihood of the life event.

Original and prevalence-based regression ranks: life events ordered by their effect on happiness. Range: 1 (most depressing) to 34 (most enhancing).

The constant: the average happiness level without any change in the independent variables. In other words, it is a measure of how happy people are on average when they are not experiencing any of the specific life events – like the births of new relatives or deaths of relatives or friends – found to impact on happiness. 2 = 'on average felt the same as usual'. The actual constant of 2.25 means that people usually thought that they felt slightly happier than average! Range: 1–3.

Regression analysis: a method for estimating the relationships between a dependent variable ('subjective happiness') and independent variables ('life events').

OLS regression equation: because the data are from samples, not a population, we have to obtain what are called ordinary least squares (OLS) estimators of the parameters.

The first line in plain English: we find that ending a close relationship – by divorce or separation, or the end of cohabitation, or ending your relationship with your boyfriend or girlfriend – has the most significant effect on reducing your level of happiness. But because this does not happen very often, it is only the sixth most likely thing to adversely affect your level of happiness.

General comment: regression analysis can trump just looking at line graph correlations, and it is an important part of toolkits for formulating and evaluating policy. It does not imply direct causation, but it highlights the strongest associations.

needs. Its most famous description appeared in a paper by the American psychologist Abraham Maslow, published during World War II.[29]

Given that Maslow was writing in 1940s America, it is perhaps unsurprising that he concentrated on the individual – with the relationship between the individual and society being implied. He came up with a hierarchy that started with basic physical needs and moved on up to safety, love, esteem and, finally, self-actualization: to realize your apparent potential and be all that you can be.

In fact, 'other people' matter most in determining our happiness. The event most strongly related to being less happy than average is the ending of a close relationship. The single event most strongly related to being happy is starting a new relationship. It is hardly surprising that most popular songs are about love. But we'll get on to love later, because if you look down the list in table 1, you'll see that sorrow associated with love is just as important as the start of a new relationship.

Combined, the death of parents (1), or of any others around you (2), and your own health (3) actually matter more in aggregate than splitting up with someone. It is just that those three events are separated in the table. Similarly, the four types of pregnancy (mine, my child's, someone else's in my family, and another's), when combined, matter more than starting a new relationship with someone.

Maslow's hierarchy of needs

19

Even though births and deaths are becoming more spread out in time, they matter more in aggregate to our happiness than starting and ending relationships with our partners – an event that has become more frequent, because more people marry more than once, and, on average, have a greater number of exclusive relationships during their lifetimes than their parents did.[30]

The table's results suggest that what matters most to us in aggregate is the health of those around us, our health, and the births and deaths of relatives and friends. We easily forget that the most valuable thing we have is our health and the health of others around us. People die on average at an older age than they used to, fewer children are born per couple, and we enjoy much better physical (if not mental) health than our parents or grandparents. And yet, *even given all that*, these events are still those that most prevent us from being happy or that most often make us more than 'reasonably' happy. What matters most to us as human beings does not change quickly.

It is easier today *not* to think about death because it is shielded from us, hidden away in hospitals and homes for the elderly. Death is also hidden in miscarriages that we don't speak about; just as being unable to have a child is hidden from polite conversation. On aggregate, it makes people very happy to start a family, even if they don't always anticipate this, and it also makes grandparents very happy. However, bringing up a family does not appear to make parents happier than other adults while they are doing it (although that may vary by country, as it can be easier in some places where childcare and good schooling is more easily accessible and free).

We are also especially good at forgetting pain: a beneficial trait in itself, but it may make us underestimate sorrow. If I had never seen the table above I would not have been able to write about how important births and deaths still are, despite knowing from my own life how much they matter. I believed issues such as 'the economy', 'the NHS' or 'immigration' mattered the most, because I have read so many news reports on opinion polls. We are overloaded with polling information where newspaper editors chose the questions that pollsters ask, and it makes us think that we are odd if we place too much emphasis on things that – according to polls – are not seen by others as important.

It is normal to be most concerned with the mountainous problem that is immediately in front of you – no matter how insignificant a molehill it might later appear. Taking a driving test, for example. It took me five attempts to pass. It was the hardest and most stressful test I ever took. In hindsight I am very grateful to all those instructors who failed me, because I am still here and have not hit and injured anyone else. I now mostly cycle, partly because I know how likely (eventually very likely) it is that I will be involved in a crash if I drive – I happen to know the odds because I read the work of those who calculate them.[31] (People have worked out the odds on almost everything, some intriguing and some amusing. For instance, you can easily find out how likely you are to have sex given your age, where you live and your gender – but for that you will have to buy another book.[32])

Although it appears in the base layer of Maslow's hierarchy, 'sex' didn't feature at all in the list of most important things that happened to people in the past twelve months. Maybe it didn't matter that much, maybe we are a little prudish, or maybe other things mattered more when we looked back. The least significant event that just registers as statistically significant enough to be included here is passing your driving test. Passing your driving test is far harder than having sex. We mostly only do it once (pass a driving test, that is), not all of us do it, and it only just shows up as having a significant effect on our overall happiness. In table 1, it is the most significant element of the 'thing' labelled as: 'Other event (10–11, 32–34,37–39,90–95)' (see the appendix at the end of this book for what those numbers mean). Much else that is more trivial than passing a driving test matters, but not enough, and not to enough of us at the same time, to register when undertaking a study of this type.

There will be a great many things that this analysis leaves out. For example, it is possible that something as simple as the people around us smiling matters to our happiness, and many other everyday events that we are not aware of could be correlated to being happier than usual. But we don't record a stranger smiling as a significant event when asked. It is possible that frequently being ignored matters greatly to us, but again we don't recognize that as an event other than in saying 'nothing happened'. Having a particular set of beliefs that you hold that get you through life might matter. But as the full title of the table says, it is a regression analysis using pooled data from waves of surveys – nothing more, nothing less.

Incidentally, that 'constant' of 2.25 matters quite a lot. The constant is a measure of peoples' average recorded happiness level when they are not experiencing any of the specific life events mentioned as being of any significance, such as births or deaths. This shows that we tend to lean towards the optimistic. A value of 2 would indicate that the average response to the question of whether we are feeling reasonably happy is to reply 'same as usual'. In fact, more of us reply 'more so than usual'. In other words, we think we are – on average – more happy than usual. Unfortunately, this may be a bad thing in the wider scheme of things because we cannot on average be happier than average … and we may overestimate how well we are doing compared with what might be possible; but more on that later.[33]

In between nothing of any importance happening to you (the most likely thing) and passing your driving test (the rarest event that shows up in the analysis) is much of the rest of life's rich tapestry: some thirty-two possible other events. Some are not that unusual, such as taking a holiday; others are profound, including experiencing the death of a loved one. They all matter and, importantly, it matters that they are not all that surprising.

The single event that on its own makes us happiest is starting a relationship. Getting hired to do a new job is the next most rewarding experience. Happiness can be fleeting; changes of state can make us happiest. But before we get to what makes us most happy, let's worry about what damages our happiness the most.

Death

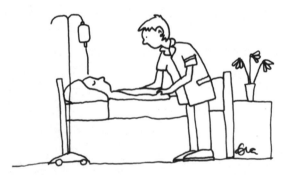

What makes us most unhappy is the ending of a relationship, and – in aggregate – we become most unhappy upon the ending of relationships as a result of death. Most common is the death of a parent. For most of us, when they die, our parents are the people we have known the longest. However, just because it is a predictable event does not mean that we will deal with it well when it occurs.

People in the UK are living longer and longer, but recently there has been a drop in life expectancy for women aged over sixty. The drop was 'only' five weeks in length, but five weeks for the average older woman is the equivalent to the average harm caused if all women in Britain were to smoke an additional 9,163 cigarettes during their lives. This is because each cigarette takes 11 minutes off your life on average.[34] For women aged over eighty-five, the group for whom the recent rise in mortality was first recorded, there has been a drop of 2.5 months in life expectancy in just two years. The number of deaths rose abruptly in 2015, so these statistics will worsen.

Could it be that the rise in smoking in the past has led to more of our mothers and grandmothers dying a little earlier? Unnamed experts talking to *The Telegraph* said that 'the trend could be the result of changes in the lifestyles of the "baby boomer" generation, with older women more likely to drink regularly, and to have smoked, than previous generations'.[35] But for this to be true, there would have had to have been a remarkably rapid take-up of cigarettes among women in the past, especially among older women. It turns out that these deaths were not due to lung cancer or similar causes, and neither were the additional deaths due to flu.[36]

Speculation – yet to be confirmed – suggests that this rise in deaths among elderly women is related to the impact of austerity in the UK. In other words, when home visits to those known to be vulnerable were cut, when pensioner income credit was reduced, and when residential homes were struggling, the frailest of the elderly were more likely to die a little earlier. One director of public health that I spoke to described impoverished elderly women living on their own as 'the canaries in the mine'. There were tens of thousands of women who died a little too early in Britain in 2012, 2013 and almost certainly through to 2016, although data for the past two years has yet to be released.[37]

The fact that the rise in mortality was much higher for elderly women than for men perhaps gives us a clue. Elderly women are much more likely than elderly men to be living on their own. Men die on average earlier than women, and usually marry women a few years younger than themselves. Men are also usually much better off (financially) than women in old age.

As well as being more likely to be poor and to live alone, women in the UK have borne the brunt of austerity measures. Some 85% of the cuts to benefits have already been taken from women – around £22 billion in the period 2010–14 – and the cuts are projected to rise rapidly in the 2015–19 period.[38] Almost the entire UK government deficit is to be repaid through sacrifices made by women. Men are usually better off than women, and their pensions are higher; furthermore, women more often end up in low-paid work because of care responsibilities, which is one reason that they get worse pensions. A group of largely male politicians decided that women should bear most of the burden of cuts.

Preventing the deaths of young people is often seen as much more important than preventing avoidable mortality among the frail and old. And yet even if you agree with that, you should stop and think about those who are left behind. Because people do care about deaths. Peoples' happiness plummets most when others close to them die. The vast majority of deaths are of the very elderly.

Think about how you might end up if you are lucky enough to die old. Let me say that again, because people don't like to think about this, and that might be part of our more general political problem. In what sort of a society, with what kind of care, do you want to end up? Do you want your relatives to have time to visit you, or would you rather they were working all available hours to perform better economically? Do you want the people who are caring for you towards the end of your life to be worrying more about how they will pay their own bills on their low income or worrying more about you? Will you end up feeling like a burden to everyone around you?

The vast majority of the deaths that we experience are of people older than us: our grandparents, and then our parents. Despite the predictability of most deaths, they shock us deeply. The death of a parent is almost as damaging to our happiness as the end of a relationship with a partner. It is the second most damaging life event of all the thirty-four discussed here in terms of its effect on our happiness. We need fewer deaths among the young, more 'good deaths'[39] of those older than us, and a better way of coming to terms with death generally. That is not what we have had in recent years. Even the very rich often have bad, lonely deaths in the UK.[40]

The hardest deaths to cope with are those for which there is little warning, and when people die out of the expected age order. The saddest deaths recorded are those of grandchildren by grandparents, and of children by parents. These are the rarest but they result in the greatest drop in happiness. The deaths of the young are also the most preventable, and preventing them has much wider benefits to family and friends than any cost–benefit model ever measures, because of their wider ramifications.

In the UK we tolerate much higher death rates among the young than are tolerated in the rest of Western Europe. Perhaps we are not so good at understanding how important mutual care, compassion, solidarity and cooperation are? The US has the highest infant mortality rate in the rich world because so many parents there bring children into the world while in poverty. In the UK we do not do much better.

Around 6,000 children die each year in the UK, mostly when very young. In 2014 a paper in The Lancet explained that the UK was in the worst section of the Western European league table for both infant and child mortality, and below 'countries including Cyprus, Greece, Spain and Portugal and ... more in line with Poland and Serbia than with the high performing countries such as Iceland, Sweden and Germany'.[41] Perhaps people in the UK don't care much about it. Maybe we think these deaths almost always occur to other peoples' children, and we don't worry as much about other people as those in other affluent countries do? Infant death rates are highest within the UK in the poorest inner cities and in Northern Ireland. In all of the rest of Europe, only parents in Romania and Malta see more of their infants die.[42]

The UK has the highest level of economic inequality – the widest differences between rich and poor – in Europe. The best-off 10% in the UK take 28% of national income, a larger share than in any other European country. This gap is almost entirely due to the best-off 1% in the UK taking such a large slice of the cake.[43] People in more economically unequal countries trust each other less and think of many others around them as less deserving. Lower trust and greater inequality move together hand in hand.[44] It is because of how we organize our society that, for every one hundred children born, twice as many children die in childhood in the UK than in Sweden. There were no causes of death that were significantly more frequent in Sweden than in the UK.[45] How society is organized affects all causes of death, from infection to congenital malformation to car crashes.

In affluent countries, the most common cause of sudden death of children, young adults and the elderly is to be hit by a car. In fact it is now widely agreed that the word 'accident' should no longer be used to describe these deaths, as in aggregate they are very predictable. Children in the UK are twice as likely to be killed when crossing the road as those in France, Norway or the Netherlands.[46] None of these individual deaths is 'expected', but the number is very predictable year on year, as is the effect on surviving family and friends. Similarly, it is also a devastating shock when people kill themselves or die from drug poisoning or overdoses. Despite recent rises in the relevant figures, these deaths continue to surprise, and destroy, families. Because the chances of such an event at any one time are rare, we tend to discount the overall risk and burden. We also dislike talking about mental illness. Because of this, as a society, we ignore too much avoidable suffering. Of the eleven affluent countries for which comparable statistics exist, we in the UK are second only to the US in terms of the frequency of mental illness.[47]

However, in other measures (such as suicide rates) we fare better than other countries. There is nothing inevitable about these rankings. Murders, for example, are much rarer in the UK than in the US, for the obvious reason that guns are far harder to obtain in the UK. What little gun crime there is in the UK is more commonly found in the countryside than in the city.[48] The suicide rate in the UK, although rising, is much lower than in France, where a higher rate of suicides has been tolerated for longer.[49]

However, suicide remains the leading single cause of death for those aged 25–49, accounting for 26% of the deaths of all men who die in the UK between the ages of 20 and 34 (and 13% of women in that age range), and of a further 13% of all men who die by age 49.[50] The absolute numbers who die due to suicide are higher in the forties than at any other point in life. All else being equal, our happiness levels tend to fall as we grow older and gain more responsibilities, regrets and recriminations; but they then rise again after our forties. We then begin to appreciate our blessings more and dwell less on misfortunes.[51]

In other causes of death not due to disease, the UK also fares poorly. Of thirty-two European countries, the UK has the fourth highest rate of drug-induced death amongst those aged 15–64, and that was before recent rises in UK drug-related deaths.[52] In September 2015 it was reported that 3,346 people in England and Wales had died as a result of drug poisoning in the year 2014. This is the highest number since records began, and two-thirds of those deaths involved illegal drugs.[53] There was a 64% increase in deaths involving heroin and/or morphine in England and Wales between 2012 and 2014. That is an unprecedented increase in such a short time. Why do so many more people become addicted to drugs in the UK than in many other affluent countries, and why is the rate rising now? Deaths involving cocaine rose by 46% over the same period. Figures for 2015 will not be available until late in 2016.

Politicians often dislike coroners commenting on the underlying social and political causes of excess premature mortality. The reaction of the government to the news of rising mortality in 2015 was to say:

> Any death related to drugs is a tragedy... Our drugs strategy is about helping people get off drugs and stay off them for good, and we will continue to help local authorities give tailored treatment to users.[54]

Yet, at the same time, local authority budgets were being cut, and cut again. One result has been the loss of much valuable local collective experience of dealing with drug addiction. In November 2015 one local resident of Oxfordshire wrote to the council complaining about the extent of the cuts to local services, saying he could not understand why services were being cut when funding had only had a 'slight fall'. The Conservative leader of Oxfordshire County Council wrote back to him to explain that the fall was £72 million, or 37% of local budgets, and was not 'slight'. The resident in question was the prime minister, David Cameron.[55]

Dealing with what life throws at us individually is very different from dealing with it on a collective basis. None of us can completely protect ourselves from pain, or ensure we maximize our happiness and minimize our suffering at all times. But we can work together to increase our overall well-being and minimize the risk of the harm that could befall any of us. We can ensure that services exist in case we or our friends or family need them, but instead we voted to cut council budgets, reduce rehabilitation assistance for drug addicts, and cut social service visits to elderly people, harming most those that live on their own.

Other affluent countries take reducing mortality more seriously. For example, in 1997 the Swedish parliament introduced a policy called 'Vision Zero' that required avoidable deaths and serious injuries on Swedish roads to be reduced to zero by the year 2020, and it commanded government to ensure that it happens.[56] In other countries road networks are built to minimize traffic crashes. The worth of a human life is set many times higher in their cost–benefit analyses of new underpasses and bridges, or in decisions over what speed traffic should be slowed down to. Public transport systems are promoted because they are far safer, and more cycling and walking are encouraged. Not so in the UK. Here we are still battling to have 20 miles per hour zones introduced into most towns and villages, in residential streets and near shops and schools. By 2030 over a quarter of the UK population will be aged over sixty-five. When hit by a car at an impact speed of 30 mph, the risk of fatality for pedestrians aged sixty or older is 47%, compared with a figure of 5% for younger adults.[57]

The stories our mortality statistics tell are all about real people and communities; they are not just abstract statistics. In 2014 two pensioners were killed on the A49 road near Church Stretton in Shropshire, an area with a population of 4,700. These deaths were reported as having had:

> a large impact on this small town, affecting many people and extending well beyond the boundaries of close family and friends. Both of those killed were well known and both were physically active and going about their normal everyday tasks.[58]

As more of us die in old age, more of us may want to have more control over how, and exactly when, we will die. Deaths affect the living in detrimental ways more than any other major influence on self-reported levels of happiness. We should care more about surviving friends and family than we currently do. Government should include estimates of the harm done to the lives of surviving friends and relatives in its calculations of whether it is worth designing safer roads and making other policies less harmful and more helpful.[59]

Across the UK today, small campaigning groups are working to reverse the rising trends in drug overdoses, in road deaths, in early childhood mortality and in preventable deaths amongst the elderly. The reason they give for their work is simple: the effects on those who are left behind, on the survivors.[60] We don't like to talk about death, but death matters. We should learn from the countries where earlier and sudden deaths are rarer than in the UK.

We urgently need to ascertain why there has been a recent reduction in life expectancy among the elderly in the UK, especially among women.

We need to prioritize actions that reduce the number of sudden deaths among young people. Specifically, the prevention of road deaths and deaths from drugs must become a focus of urgent importance. We need to look at other countries to understand why our children are now among the most likely to die young in all of Europe.

We need to talk more about suicide – because among those entering middle age it is now the most common cause of death.

We need to think more about good deaths and good, long lives.

Illness

When more people fall ill, the demands on doctors grow, especially in poorer areas where local services are run down. Four out of every five hospital consultants in the UK were considering early retirement in 2015. Two out of five work overtime every week, all year, without fail. One NHS consultant's experience is characteristic of recent changes and experiences:

> For the first time in my life on anti-depressants ... it affected my sleep... [I am] not very tolerant with kids... [I am] unable to support them through GCSEs and A-levels ... due to stresses at work.[61]

Nurses and other health workers report similar fatigue, and have far lower incomes than consultants. Social workers, old age home carers, porters, paramedics: all are seeing their standard of living fall as wages in the public sector are frozen and as tax credits are removed. When those looking after our health are becoming more anxious and less healthy themselves, the rest of us cannot be cared for so well. Both in the NHS and beyond it, the majority of carers are women, who live longer than men, but who also live longer in ill health.

In winter 2015 a junior doctor who works in the accident and emergency department of an NHS hospital wrote to me. She told me that sometimes the only thing she could do that was actually of use was spend time with a patient, listening. But that is incompatible with the four-hour target to discharge people, so staff end up passing 'complicated' patients around the NHS. In November 2015 the Organisation for Economic

Co-Operation and Development (OECD) explained that the UK needed an extra 47,700 nurses and 26,500 doctors to be able to match provision in France, Canada, Belgium, Germany, New Zealand and Denmark. At an annual cost of £5 billion a year, this would require higher taxation,[62] but it would allow better staffing levels at weekends, in August and during other holiday periods.

Putting extra money into hospitals makes little difference, though, if they can't discharge patients because there is no social care available locally, which is the case in many areas. Mental health funding cuts leave more people in hospital beds because it is not safe for them to go home. Among the population as a whole, resilience and life skills are declining; front-line accident and emergency services are now replacing general health education. The doctor who explained all of this to me in her letter said that the NHS needed more funding in public health to prevent future healthcare being overwhelmed. She was young and enthusiastic, not burnt out like so many of her older colleagues. However, despite being a doctor, she could only just pay her rent in a shared house. All around her, services were being offered for tender to the lowest bid from any private provider.

As American astronaut John Glenn once said of the experience of being launched into space, 'I feel about as good as anybody would, sitting in a capsule on top of a rocket that were both built by the lowest bidder'. Being cared for in old age in a care home that is being run at the lowest possible cost, being looked after by people who can find no other work – people who leave their jobs as fast as they can get a better one – what kind of an old age will that be?

As yet, the freezing of NHS funds at current levels ('ring-fencing') is not being suggested as a major reason for the rising mortality rates among some groups in the UK. However, part of what is going wrong in the short term is that the Department of Work and Pensions (DWP), which is separate from the NHS, requires its staff, especially those at a relatively junior level, to make daily decisions about individuals that could directly harm their health. The DWP publishes guidance for Job Centre officials who decide whether claimants who may have infringed rules should have their payments stopped.

> The guidance says: it would be usual for a normal healthy adult to suffer some deterioration in their health if they were without:
> 1. Essential items such as food, clothing, heating and accommodation, or
> 2. Sufficient money to buy essential items for a period of two weeks.
> The Decision Maker must decide if the health of the person with the medical condition would decline more than a normal healthy adult.[63]

Research published at the end of 2015 demonstrated that for every 10,000 assessments the DWP undertakes in just one of the programmes designed to cut benefits (the Work Capability Assessment), an additional 7,020 antidepressants have to be prescribed and an additional six suicides result. In the four-year period 2010–13, some 1.03 million existing claimants were reassessed (3% of the working-age population). The number of suicides associated with this programme was 590, and the number of additional antidepressants prescribed was 725,000.[64] These numbers will be far higher by the time you read this; with every single number representing an individual story of tragedy.[65] All the while, hundreds of thousands of people receiving government-sponsored 'psychological preparation' sessions,[66] supposedly to make them 'work ready', are being repeatedly given demeaning messages such as: 'Nobody ever drowned in sweat.'[67]

We choose how much we prioritize our health and well-being over competing commitments. In other countries in Europe more is spent on welfare and health. Health spending per person is 49% higher in Germany, 41% higher in Denmark and 27% higher in France than it is in the UK.[68] In addition to spending more on health, most other countries in Europe are willing to put more health warnings on food items that contain a lot of sugar (or levy a sugar tax), or to have alcohol taxes that are higher than ours. They also use tax revenues to pay for better collective social security than is offered in the UK.[69]

In contrast, UK government officials are now being instructed (as the guidance quotation directly above makes clear) to expect people's health to deteriorate as a result of the 'discretionary' social security sanctions that are being applied. This should itself cause us to realize that there is something very wrong at the heart of our politics. As an emeritus professor of law in Scotland explained in October 2015: 'Benefit sanctions, as they have developed in the UK, are incompatible with justice.'[70]

The sanctions affect some groups receiving benefits far more than others and so will cause illness, especially mental illness, to rise more among those groups. Women with care responsibilities are disproportionately sanctioned for not attending Job Centre appointments:

> Women are being expected to meet near impossible conditions in order to receive a basic benefit. When those conditions aren't met these women are sanctioned, often losing all of their benefits – sometimes repeatedly – as the result of a system that doesn't take account of the specific circumstances of many women's lives.[71]

Almost all of these women are caring for children, who also suffer.

Welfare should not be a weapon, and its withdrawal should not be used as a form of punishment. You would not punish people by withdrawing their access to healthcare, so why is it acceptable to punish them by withdrawing social security payments and, hence, access to food? Why target women more than men, children more than adults? Our welfare system is miserly in comparison with those in most other European countries, which results in more premature mortality and illness in the UK, which in turn spreads fear, mistrust and unhappiness into the wider population.

It is very important to remember that the deaths of others cause us the most unhappiness, when measured across the population as a whole, closely followed by the ill health of our loved ones. This is especially true when it comes to the poor health of our parents, which affects most of us much more than our own ill health (which we adapt to). Most of us are fairly healthy, and we are likely to live through the declining health of our parents. Illness amongst our children, although more rare, is especially hurtful. It is worth repeating that this is particularly so for grandparents, who do not expect to outlive their grandchildren. In contrast, achieving good health and being well-treated results in significant rises in happiness.

Watching those around us suffer as welfare benefits are withdrawn harms us even if we are ourselves better off. Watching our friends and neighbours being unable to pay the rent, or seeing them become ill from worry or from cold as they turn down the heating, hurts. Even if we can pay our way, it hurts us to see others suffer. So we try not to look. But as Professor John Middleton, England's longest serving director of public health,[72] explained in November 2015: 'Health professions deal every day with the victims of welfare failure and a sick food system.'[73] Food is at the base of Maslow's hierarchy of needs. Some community doctors in the UK now issue vouchers from local food banks in addition to prescribing medicines.

We are not focusing enough on the issues that make us most unhappy in this most unequal of affluent societies. Table 2 provides data on inequality and health outcomes in some of the world's most affluent nations. The US is a stark outlier: the most unequal large rich nation in the world has both a considerably higher rate of infant mortality and lower overall life expectancy than any other affluent nation. Data on mental ill health is not included in the table because comparable data for most of these countries is not available, and this lack of information must surely limit the willingness of policymakers to tackle these illnesses. In the UK today, around one in four people suffers from mental illness. Mental health disorders must not be overlooked by health policy, despite the difficulty of their measurement.[74] Somewhat easier to measure is the huge gap in household incomes between the poorest tenth of households and the richest.

In the UK the poorest tenth of households, even after adjustment for household size, receive just 2.7% of all income (after benefits are included and taxes taken away). This is less than 10% as much as the best-off tenth of households in the UK, who have recourse to 28% of all disposable income. Among the twenty-five most affluent countries in the world with a population of at least 2 million people, only in the US and Singapore do the best-off 10% take a higher proportion of total national income. Greece, Spain and Italy now look as unequal as the UK because of cuts to the living standards of the poorest people under austerity. Contrast these countries with Finland, Slovenia and Denmark to see the other political possibilities and choices as to what level of inequality to tolerate. In December 2015 the Finnish government suggested it would pilot a basic living wage of £576 per citizen per month for its resident population.[75]

More equitable affluent countries tend to have lower infant mortality rates than those of more unequal countries. Table 2 makes clear that no other affluent country in Europe has infant mortality rates as high as the UK's. Elsewhere in the rich world, only Canada, New Zealand and the US match or exceed the UK rate. The picture is much less clear when it comes to comparing life expectancy, which reflects many factors, influenced by what has happened to a population over decades, including immigration or emigration of those that are fitter and healthier. Infant mortality and mental illness are more highly correlated to inequality because they are influenced far more quickly in reaction to some immediate change in circumstances.

The first column in table 2 shows income inequality between the highest-income and lowest-income decile groups of households, with the countries being ranked

Table 2. Income inequality in affluent nations, infany mortality, life expectancy and income shares.

Country	1st-to-10th ratio (household income)	Infant mortality rate (per 1000)	Life expectancy in years, in 1990, 2000 and 2013 (and overall change)	Household income share (%)	
				1st decile group	10th decile group
United States	18.75	7	75, 77, 79 (+4)	1.60	30.00
Singapore	17.63	3	75, 79, 83 (+8)	1.64	28.97
Israel	15.06	4	77, 79, 82 (+5)	1.70	25.60
Greece	12.55	4	77, 78, 81 (+4)	2.00	25.10
Spain	11.62	4	77, 79, 83 (+6)	2.10	24.40
Italy	11.23	4	77, 80, 83 (+6)	2.20	24.70
United Kingdom	10.37	5	76, 78, 81 (+5)	2.70	28.00
Portugal	9.96	4	74, 77, 81 (+5)	2.60	25.90
South Korea	9.95	4	72, 76, 82 (+10)	2.20	21.90
Japan	8.84	3	79, 81, 84 (+5)	2.91	25.71
Australia	8.71	4	77, 80, 83 (+6)	2.80	24.40
Canada	8.64	5	77, 79, 82 (+5)	2.80	24.20
New Zealand	8.29	6	76, 79, 82 (+6)	3.10	25.70
Ireland	7.44	4	75, 77, 82 (+7)	3.40	25.30
France	7.44	4	78, 79, 82 (+4)	3.20	23.80
Austria	6.97	4	76, 78, 81 (+5)	3.10	21.60
Switzerland	6.63	4	78, 80, 83 (+5)	3.50	23.20
Netherlands	6.59	4	77, 78, 81 (+4)	3.40	22.40
Germany	6.53	4	76, 78, 81 (+5)	3.60	23.50
Sweden	6.26	3	78, 80, 82 (+4)	3.50	21.90
Norway	6.24	3	77, 79, 82 (+5)	3.30	20.60
Belgium	5.78	4	76, 78, 80 (+4)	3.60	20.80
Finland	5.51	3	75, 78, 81 (+6)	3.90	21.50
Slovenia	5.41	3	74, 76, 80 (+6)	3.70	20.00
Denmark	5.20	4	75, 77, 80 (+5)	4.00	20.80

Note: the 1st-to-10th ratio is the ratio of the mean (after tax) household income of the top decile group in a population to that of the bottom decile group, adjusted to take account of household size. Infant mortality is as reported by the World Bank (2015), and life expectancy is as reported by the World Health Organisation (2015) for both men and women combined. Global Health Observatory data repository, accessed November 2015 (http://bit.ly/1pcf4aB).

Source: N. Stotesbury and D. Dorling. 2015. Understanding income inequality and its implications: why better statistics are needed. *Statistics Views*, 21 October. (See http://bit.ly/20BOEkd.)

by that ratio. For instance, in the UK the highest-income tenth of households receive 10.37 times more income than the lowest-income tenth: 28% compared with 2.7%. In the US the highest-income tenth take 30%, compared with 1.6% for the lowest-income decile. By 2013, the lowest life expectancy in the rich world (the 3rd column) was in the US, with 79, but very equitable Denmark, Slovenia and Belgium were only a year ahead (all at 80), the UK (at 81) was just a year ahead of them, just below Norway and Sweden (at 82) and Switzerland, Australia, Italy, Spain and Singapore (all at 83), with Japan heading the list at 84, five years ahead of the US. In the twenty-three years to 2013, life expectancy in the US increased by only four years. Some nineteen countries in the table did better, five achieved the same increase, and none performed any worse than the US. Part of the reason for this is that infant mortality is often highest in those affluent countries where the richest tenth take over a quarter of all household income, as the richest are usually families without very young children.

Human beings are intrinsically and primarily self-regarding, just like other species. Self-regard is a neutral concept, not a critical one. Like other species, humans may adopt more collective behaviours if they have benefits for themselves and their kin. Often what benefits the collective also benefits the individual. Of course, we are all very different, with a wide range of sexualities and ethnicities, practising no religion or one of many possible ones. In accepting others who are not similar to us, humans have achieved a great deal of success, and many of these successes are becoming more frequent over time; but by accepting others as equal, we accept them as being like us in another way, in the respect they deserve, in the chances they should have, and in how they should be treated, not least when they (and we) are ill.

A better politics of illness and health would be a politics that did not tolerate government officials being instructed to carry out acts that they knew would damage health.

We should ensure that our National Health Service is in the future funded at the normal European level by raising more tax.

We should introduce preventative taxation, such as on sugar in foodstuffs. We should also look more carefully at the underlying causes of poor health, and at how accepting higher levels of poor health in the overall population harms the long-term happiness of us all.

Births

A better politics would not only concentrate on preventing harm – it would also promote happiness. Births are greeted by substantial increases in happiness for the new parents and grandparents, at least in the year that follows (this happiness 'spike' flattens out later as we age and the pressure of parenting kicks in). But many people who desperately wish to be parents are currently prevented from getting help. Fertility treatment in the UK is a postcode lottery. Although services are commissioned centrally in Wales, Scotland and Northern Ireland, in England fertility treatment depends on where you live and the current policy of your local Clinical Commissioning Group. Groups in poorer areas, with greater demands on general health services, are more likely to find that budget limitations oblige them to cut family planning and fertility services, including services to prevent unwanted pregnancies and the spread of sexually transmitted diseases.

Government policy in the UK now means that if any family has a third or subsequent child after April 2017 they will receive no tax credits or any universal credit benefits for those children. The Children's Society, a national children's charity, explained that this was another government measure targeted at the poorest families: 'The announcement to limit child tax credits to two children is effectively a two child policy for the poorest families.' The government's Secretary of State for Work and Pensions, Iain Duncan Smith, proposed in 2012 to cut the income of 584,000 poor families with an adult in work.[76] The Chancellor, who three years later introduced this measure in his 2015 budget, said that:

> Britain is home to 1% of the world's population; gener-
> ates 4% of the world's income; and yet pays out 7% of
> the world's welfare spending. It is not fair to the tax-
> payers paying for it. It needs to change.[77]

However, the Chancellor misled us when he implied that these three proportions are comparable and that such a comparison is meaningful.

Britain is home to only half of one per cent of the world's children, but that does not mean we are having too few children. We have *fewer* children because we are *more* affluent; we also spend more on welfare because we are more affluent than the vast majority of other countries. However, Britain has one of the *lowest* levels of welfare spending in the rich world because its taxes are very low. Rather than being unfair to taxpayers, the current situation is unfair to most children, and to the majority of adults. It benefits the richest, who avoid paying the tax they would pay if they lived elsewhere in Europe. For decades people in the UK and in every other country in Europe have been having families that are, on average, so small that our population would quickly decline were it not for immigration. There is no need to curtail the opportunity to become a parent in the UK unless you hold strange eugenic ideas.

It is harder for people to become parents in Britain today than at any time in the country's history. The cost of housing has accelerated since the economic crash, helped in part by government policies, such as 'Help to

Buy', that were introduced in the immediate aftermath of the crash.[78] It is not just poorer potential parents who cannot now afford children – it is the vast majority of young adults. Most can no longer countenance becoming parents before their thirties.

Britain does not have a surplus of children. Since 2011 the mean age of first becoming a parent has risen each year, accelerating to the point that by 2014 it had passed thirty for women and was even older for men. The number of babies born each year began to fall more rapidly after 2013 as a result.[79] There is no longer anywhere in Europe where fertility is at 'replacement level'.[80] Every country in Europe requires immigration to sustain its population level, its economy, its public services and its pension system. Policies to aid parenthood need not be altered that significantly, but we should avoid polices that make it harder for those who want to have children. Some 54,000 women are forced out of their jobs each year in the UK as a result of becoming a parent.[81] Maternity pay and paternity leave have been improved in recent years, but many people now work on short-term or zero-hours contracts and so they do not benefit from these provisions. The greatest rise in employment is in self-employment, and there is no access to security such as parental leave for most people for this rapidly growing group of workers.

To feel able to have children, people need stability. We need to not be forced to work every hour we can just

49

to get by – or, conversely, to feel under pressure to put a career first and earn as much as possible before having a child. We need to be able to imagine cutting down on the amount of paid work we do for a few years when a child is very small, and to have affordable childcare nearby, but most of all we need to know that it is OK to become a parent, and that it is not some selfish act we should engage in only if we can afford it. None of us would be here now if some of our forebears who 'could not afford it' had not become parents despite the odds. Every one of us has ancestors who were poor. And when others around us have children, and take parental leave, we need to recognize that they are not disadvantaging us by doing so, just as we are not disadvantaged by having to collectively fund the education of their children.

To be able to become parents with less fear, young adults also need to have truly affordable housing available in which they can start families. This is much more important than access to childcare, as are stable jobs; but an extension of affordable childcare is vital too, starting before the age of five, when children begin primary school.

Housing is discussed in more detail in the next chapter, but it matters in this context. If housing is made cheaper, then having a family, among other things, becomes easier. That rare thing, a secure tenancy, should be obtainable by all, including would-be parents. The government would simply need to change the law on assured short-hold tenancies so that any new ones issued must be for at least three years, or five years if a family has children. As the tenancies are currently renewed each year, such a law change would not need to be retrospective. Throughout the rest of Europe housing is cheaper, the quality of housing is often higher, rooms are larger, landlords make smaller profits, and the highest-income tenth own a smaller proportion of the housing stock (see table 2 above). [82]

If employment is more secure and stable too, then parenthood is also easier to countenance earlier. Employment can be made more secure by using legislation to ensure that redundancy payments and out-of-work benefits are on a level similar to those in other countries in Northwest Europe, not lower, as is the case today. That reduces the chances of infertility, as people do not delay pregnancy when they have more secure employment earlier on, or when they fear the consequences of unemployment less. And both the human and financial costs of attempts to overcome infertility, and the heartache it causes, are then reduced.

Just a few decades from now, people without children may well be labelled as burdens on the state. Setting aside the use of such a charged term, taking care of older people who do not have family support costs the state more than supporting young families would now. Having children saves money on mental health costs in the long run. This is because people with kids are less lonely and depressed. Beyond the workplace, a significant part of the social networks of many adults comes through friendships with the parents of other children in nurseries and schools, through shared celebrations and shared caring. Children are among the most effective socializing agents for both younger adults and the elderly.

How many people will there be a few decades from now living in their old age, unhappy? Some will be those who were so busy trying to keep up with the materialist society we live in that they had little time for anything else. How many will have put off, or have been forced to put off, something that was nagging in the back of their mind because most of their friends were also putting it off? And then, one by one, many of their friends and siblings found a way to become a parent while they did not. And how many suffer in silence because 'austerity' means that their local NHS literally decides it is too expensive to help them to have a child. Children should not be consumer commodities you cannot have if you cannot afford them. Children are not a cost. They are a benefit. We should appreciate life for the miracle that it is.

Chapter 3

Safety

> Nowadays people know the price of everything and the
> value of nothing.
> — *Oscar Wilde, The Picture of Dorian Gray*

After starting a new relationship and getting a new job, the third most significant single event associated with higher than usual happiness in any given year is securing a permanent home. Yet this is becoming increasingly difficult for younger people. The average age of a first-time buyer was only twenty-four in the 1960s (see figure 1). By 2012 that had risen to thirty-five, with people having to find an average deposit of £27,500.[83] Today these figures are higher still, and more and more people will have to rent into their forties and fifties. This is true even for those who have been to university and secured a good job. Most new renting involves private short-term tenancies. Today's younger generation are much less likely to have the security of accommodation their parents had.

Figure 1 uses information from the British Social Attitudes Survey to show the proportion of people by age that had a mortgage or owned their home outright each year in Britain from 1983 to 2012. Time is depicted along the x-axis of the figure, with the y-axis being age. The figure is a simplified version of a much more complicated graph that was first published in the *Telegraph* newspaper.[84]

In the distant past older people generally did not buy their home. Even as recently as 1983, a majority of those aged over fifty were renting from the local council or from the remnants of the old private rented sector. Several generations – those who grew up from the 1930s through to the 1980s – saw the quality of the housing they lived in improve. Now, council house building has ceased and the public rented housing stock has diminished as a result of the 'right to buy' policy. Today, quality improves only for a minority, while others live in increasingly overcrowded properties that are not well maintained. The worst maintenance is that by private landlords, as routinely revealed by the government's own annual survey of housing.

The mortgage market grew in the 1980s, but a new private rented market for students and young professionals also began to expand. By the 1990s there were fewer older people renting, and by the 2000s fewer still. People who had taken out mortgages in the 1980s were beginning to pay them off, but younger people were increasingly unable to get mortgages and the private

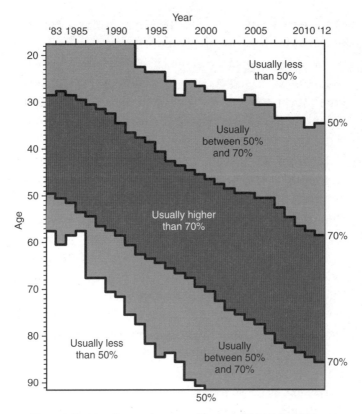

Figure 1. People with a mortgage or who own outright in the UK by age, 1983–2012 (percentage within a single year of age and year group). (Note that data are missing for 1988 and 1992; the trends have been interpolated over those two years.)

Source: analysis by the author of the British Social Attitudes Surveys.

rented sector expanded further. Then, with the crash in 2008, the mortgage market dried up for first-time buyers but boomed for buy-to-let landlords. Most people aged between twenty-five and fifty were renting again, but now mostly from private landlords.

By the early 1990s, buying a home became associated with an increase in happiness that is more than seven times the happiness boost linked with simply moving home. This is perhaps related to the fourth and fifth most significant events associated with greater happiness: becoming pregnant or your child becoming pregnant (discussed at the end of chapter 2). The arrival of a new-born often necessitates moving to a bigger property, or at least it did in the past.

So why are fewer people able to afford the security of their own homes? Why are so many finding rent so hard to pay that they know they have no hope of saving for a deposit? The inability to save, rapidly rising prices in many areas, higher profit-taking by British banks than European banks, and lower median wages in the UK all contribute to preventing people who would like to buy from doing so. It is 'investors' and landlords who are increasing their share of property ownership. We are using our existing housing stock less and less efficiently compared with more equitable European countries.[85]

In the UK council tax benefit has been cut, while rent, gas and electricity costs have gone up. The result of this is that many British households (as many as a quarter) can no longer pay for rent, fuel and food while also saving at least £10 a month. These changes affect poorer households with children the most because, relative to wealthier households, expenditure on these necessities comprises a larger percentage of their overall consumption.

People will go without food, and will then go without heat for their homes, before they fail to pay the rent. Yet in London the number of families issued with a court summons for not paying their rent doubled from 7,283 in 2013–14 to 15,509 in 2014–15.[86] There was a 50% increase in the use of bailiffs to evict households over that same period. When you are evicted, you also face £125 in court costs and £400 in bailiff's fees – in the UK you pay for your own eviction.

Over half a million children in London are now living in poverty. Half of those children are housed in the private rented sector, and that number has doubled in a matter of just a few years. When the families of those children are evicted for not paying their rent, or move on because they can no longer pay their rent as it rises, those children often have to move to another school, losing their friends and having to make new ones. Children in poverty and in private rented accommodation move, on average, more than once every three years.[87]

We cannot be happy if we do not feel safe and secure in our homes. The government has a responsibility towards the quality and quantity of housing available and it must introduce the security and quality in socially and privately rented housing that we currently lack compared with nearby countries. The government must get involved in rent regulation, and control the buying of properties by buy-to-let landlords. It must intervene in the housing market to halt the ongoing escalation of house prices. One way it could do this is by adopting Kate Barker's suggestion that capital gains tax is paid on all properties.[88]

Rents

Young professionals also now suffer from having to pay high rents to private landlords. This is causing increased angst even for them, despite this group being reasonably well off, with higher and more reliable incomes than others of their age, with supposedly bright prospects and usually no dependants. This phenomenon is best known in London, but it is also becoming prevalent in a number of other affluent cities in some of the most unequal countries of the rich world, although generally not elsewhere in Europe. London is now the most expensive very large city to live in in the world. To find a comparable situation to London, but in a smaller affluent city, you have to travel to San Francisco.

By 2015, in any neighbourhood of San Francisco, it had become impossible for a single teacher to pay the median rent on a one-bedroom apartment; the average rent in the very poorest neighbourhood there rose to $3,500 a month. Californian teachers' starting annual salaries were $50,000. After paying taxes and buying food, any teacher without recourse to wealth would inevitably find themselves in debt.[89] However, travel a third of the way round the world in the opposite direction and you come to Tokyo, where rents have fallen by over 15% in the last ten years as landlord greed is better controlled.[90] In contrast, in the UK, rents in the city of Oxford, for example, are rising rapidly and will soon exceed £1,000 a month for a one-bedroom apartment. This will leave rent consuming a large majority of a newly qualified teacher's income of £22,000 a year. Indeed, it leaves very little after taxes are deducted and clothes and food are paid for.[91] Few newly qualified teachers stay long in the city, meaning that a very large proportion of teachers in Oxford's schools are young and inexperienced.

Average UK private rental prices went above £1,000 a month during the early autumn of 2015. One-bedroom flats in London had already passed that price level in August 2015. Nationally, in 2015 rents were rising by 4.6% a year, but by 20% a year in London boroughs like Islington.[92] Part of the reason for this is landlord greed, and part of it, according to the bank UBS, is because by 2015 'London house prices [became the] most overvalued in the world'.[93]

Rising rents are 'socially cleansing' poorer people from the more expensive parts of the UK. In many London boroughs a third of poor families have had to leave their homes, their boroughs or possibly London entirely since 2010. In most cases it was the cut to housing benefit that forced them to leave. For others living across Southeast England and in other expensive areas, when households were hit by redundancy or illness or divorce, high housing costs then mattered for people who had thought they were immune. This was compounded by the introduction of the 'benefits cap', which mostly affects households with children, especially disabled children, and the unrelenting annual above-inflation rises in rents.

Jeremy Corbyn, the leader of the Labour Party, represents Islington North, an area of London with one of the highest rates of poverty in Europe. He puts it bluntly:

> Frankly we're being socially cleansed. The rent goes up, the benefit cap doesn't meet the rent. That means [people are] either forced to go hungry or move away from their families and the lives they've built.[94]

It is possible to stop this. In Scotland, Nicola Sturgeon, the leader of the Scottish National Party, has promised to introduce local rent regulations for the private sector in 'high-pressure areas'. She has the power to do so. The old argument that rent regulation would reduce the supply and quality of rented housing appears flawed. The quality of much UK private rented accommodation is awful by normal European standards, including Eastern European standards, and the price is simply too high.[95] Making sure that minimal standards are enforced would at first most help those currently living in damp, rodent-infested, poorly insulated, dilapidated accommodation in the UK. This would save money for the NHS as well. Berlin has had successful rent regulation for years, and it has far higher quality housing as a result. The regulations were recently tightened up in Berlin to stem housing-cost inflation.

Social (and later private) housing rents should be subject to regulation, to ensure that they are not more than 30% of disposable income. Tenants such as students who might wish to leave their tenancy early could do so, but landlords could not insist that they do. If the quality of accommodation is substandard, tenants should have the right to improve it, deduct the cost from their rent, and extend their tenancies by more years in proportion to how much they had to spend. That would give the landlord an incentive to improve standards. Private renting needs to be made a reputable housing sector so that good pension companies can invest in it.

Improving tenants' terms and conditions would result in a fall in the value of property, overall, as landlords would get a lower yield from their investment. More housing still needs to be built, but in recent years the private sector has failed to deliver. Local authorities need to coordinate additional housebuilding, including planning transport links and other infrastructure. Their involvement would curtail the profits made by the current oligopoly of a few large housebuilders. The state could encourage small housebuilding projects. The private housing market is failing.

Savings

For several years the Office for National Statistics (ONS) has been monitoring both the wealth and well-being of

UK citizens. In early autumn 2015 it first published results on the effect of savings on well-being. What the ONS found was startling. It is not income that matters most to us, but having some savings:

> An individual's level of personal well-being is strongly related to the level of wealth of the household in which they live. Life satisfaction, sense of worth and happiness are higher, and anxiety less, as the level of household wealth increases. The levels of household income are less strongly related, with relationships found only with life satisfaction and sense of worth.[96]

In other words, people feel safer if they have savings they can fall back on. If wealth were more evenly distributed, far more of us could have savings and a few would not have such great fortunes. One person's personal income, through receiving an income from unprotected tenants, results in a reduction in the tenants' safety. Protect the tenants and regulate their rent and they gain a lot. The landlord loses only a little profit; total net safety increases.

In the five years from 2010, an additional 207,000 people in the UK became paper millionaires, mostly because the value of their property had risen.[97] They didn't suddenly become wealthy, because in almost all cases their wealth had been just a little short of a million pounds a few years earlier. It represented a 41% increase in millionaires in the UK in that period, and yet most simply had a property that was (in theory) worth some more, but that they still needed to live in. In the ONS survey, high levels of property wealth and private pension wealth were not found to be related to higher levels of personal well-being. It was smaller amounts of liquid wealth that correlated most strongly with higher personal well-being – savings for a rainy day. However, a quarter of households can currently save nothing at all, and another quarter can save almost nothing. Only those at the very top of the wealth parade can save a lot, and saving a lot does not make you feel much more secure than saving a modest amount.

One in every sixty-five people in the UK is now a paper millionaire,[98] but few feel they have money to burn. Above them in the wealth parade are those receiving some £42 billion in bonuses in their pay in just one year. Most of these people work in financial services, but most bankers receiving a bonus feel their bonus is small in relation to those of a few of their colleagues. And even those colleagues feel (literally) poor compared with the wealthiest 1,000 families in the UK, who have doubled their wealth holdings in the five years since 2010. Self-perceptions of wealth are all relative.

The UK is now home to the world's third-largest concentration of people whose wealth is worth over

The Wealth parade

$50 million: so-called ultra high net worth individuals. Britain ranks just below much more populous China and the US. Worldwide inequity has risen again in recent years, faster than had been expected. As the chief executive of Oxfam put it: 'Are we really happy to live in a world where the top 1% own half the wealth and the poorest half own just 1%?'[99] The global realignment of wealth away from Europe and the US will take decades. In the meantime, we need to be concerned with the next few years.

The US provides a model of what the UK may become if the rise in wealth inequalities is not curtailed. More than 3 million American households have a net wealth of between one and two million dollars, and at least a further 3 million have more than two million dollars each in assets.[100] In 2015 the 400 richest US families owned, in total, more wealth than 36 million median-wealth families did, combined.[101] Each held the same wealth as 90,000 average US families. Even the middle 20% of US households, including the median, had wealth averaging only $12,200 per household. The top 20% held more than all the rest combined.[102]

Annual wealth taxation is needed because the alternative is that a small group becomes ever wealthier to the detriment of the rest. Progressive annual property taxation would achieve a great deal, as could a simple flat tax on the value of all property owned, but even that would not be as effective as a more progressive tax based on total land value and property value. Council tax is a regressive tax that only applies to some property and not to land.

Saving small amounts should be encouraged and property speculation should be discouraged. Everyone needs some savings for a rainy day in order to feel secure. The Child Trust Fund was one government policy that tried to encourage this. It has now been cut, but it has reduced some wealth inequalities. Less inequality results in more security for all. Taxing the rich more could pay for that security, including the restoration of the Child Trust Fund.

Eviction

Safety matters. The implications of not being safe can be terrifying and harmful to our health. In just twelve months to June 2015, 43,000 households were evicted in England and Wales: the highest number ever recorded and 50% higher than the rate at the depth of the economic recession. According to the *Financial Times*, 'the situation is likely to deteriorate as a result of Chancellor George Osborne's plan to reduce the overall benefits cap'.[103] Is it any wonder that people's well-being is so influenced by some savings? You are not safe if you are poor, or of modest (or even average or mildly affluent) means in the UK today. The rich fear joining the mildly affluent and getting on that downward slope; they will try hard to avoid any fall in their wealth. The current extent of the fear is extreme, because the gaps are now so wide.

Housing is in short supply because it is now being used in ways that are more inefficient than at any time since records of our use of housing began in 1911. A higher proportion of homes are empty and more rooms in them are underused than ever before. Becky Tunstall, professor of housing policy at the University of York, has demonstrated this using data from every census up to 2011.[104] We know we did not have a large number of empty or underused homes before 1911. Almost all of this spare capacity is in the private sector, and mostly it is found among those who own outright, largely due to older homeowners holding on to large properties for the rising asset value, possibly hoping to pass that on to their children when they die. At the same time, and partly because of the increases in property hoarding that Professor Tunstall uncovered, homelessness and overcrowding are also rising.

We need to build more homes, because we currently have too few, and our population is rising due to immigration. However, the five largest building firms in the UK have a disproportionately large stake in overall housing construction. These five firms secured that advantageous position in recent years by taking over their smaller competitors, who suffered the most in the housing crash of 2008.[105] The situation we find ourselves in is very unusual and calls for new routes out of the crisis. The market has not, cannot and will not deliver enough homes to the people in most need.

The quickest way to relieve the housing crisis and reduce evictions would be to introduce policies that encourage people living alone in properties with many more rooms than they use to think sooner about downsizing and to discourage people from buying second homes as an investment. Very large properties could be subdivided into flats in future. This happened before when economic inequalities fell. Incidentally, the former chairman of the National Trust, Simon Jenkins, agrees that we are not using our existing housing well enough. But we will eventually have to build more.[106]

We will also have to build more housing because our population is rising. We have to build retirement apartments (with lifts) attractive enough for people to downsize to, not ghettos for the elderly. We have to build homes in and near cities, where people will not need cars to be able to live good lives. And we have to ensure that the value of housing begins to fall towards normal European levels so that there is a disincentive to hoard housing.

The purchase of housing as an investment should be made unaffordable by increasing taxation on empty homes and ensuring that capital gains tax applies to all property.

Already in the UK a lot of effort goes into 'prevent[ing] the eviction and repossession of vulnerable borrowers who have defaulted on their housing loan'.[107] But, in contrast, in Sweden the risk of getting into that situation in the first place is minimized by the state. In Germany people are far freer to choose between renting and buying than they are in the UK; buying in Germany has benefits but is no great investment. In the Netherlands tenancies are better controlled, so the quality of rented housing is higher and the price is lower. In France rented homes are much more spacious, on average, than in the UK. In the US property taxes are fairer. The Japanese are decades ahead of the British in terms of planning housing to fit in with public transport, so car use there has been falling for many years.

Housing in the UK needs to be for homes, not for investment. And we need to look abroad to see how to make this the case. We need to look at how housing policy in other countries has contributed to better mental health in those countries. We need to ask why we allow a tiny proportion of people to profit so much from charging such high rents and demanding such high prices for homes? Having so many people living in tenures that are so insecure does not promote well-being in a population. It spreads mistrust.

Chapter 4

Love

If there is one word that encapsulates the new sense of connection between people that seems to be emerging it is 'humanity'. The common outrage is overwhelmingly directed at its opposite – inhumanity.

— *Ursula Huws*[108]

What do people want above all else? For most people the answer is simple: other people. People to love them, occasionally hug them, always respect them and care for them, and for them to care for in return. People do not want policies that focus on maximizing profit or wealth. This is so overwhelmingly apparent that it is staggering to be told that we should consign our most important relationships to the 'private sphere'. In an age when all can be fed, kept warm and sheltered, it is shocking that we cannot supply these basics adequately to all – because of a policy focus on wealth maximization.

People have greatly valued their relationships, and feared being ostracized, since long before the words 'economic' and 'growth' had any meaning. However, it takes a strangely economistic way of measuring the world to determine this anew. This kind of strange measurement is what Dimitris Ballas and I did when we estimated what best predicted happiness (or its lack) in the model that is the evidence base for this book. Our relationships with each other are what matter most to us, but for those who like to see these things set out in numbers, here they are.

If your main relationship has ended during the past year, that will have had the highest detrimental effect on your happiness of any possible single event (this is shown in the table in chapter 2 by the single biggest negative coefficient, −0.178). The cause is usually separation or divorce. Fortunately, because separation is relatively rare, it is only the sixth most detrimental event by prevalence: that is, its impact multiplied by its likelihood. It is not so much that marriage is good for us – although getting married is – it is that splitting up is so very bad for us.

Other relationships matter too, especially with pets – which are much more important than we tend to give them credit for. Something that negatively affects a pet is the fifteenth most detrimental event overall, or seventeenth by prevalence. Pets tend to leave our social circle a little more often than long-term human partners, mostly because cats and dogs have short life expectancies.

Relationships with the rest of your family (pets aside) are frequently mentioned, but often for making people less 'reasonably' happy than usual, such as after a family event. When you last met up with your family did you all sing round the piano? Or did you drink and eat too much and try to avoid an argument? But what is key to understanding ourselves is that our relationships with others figure as more important than anything else in our lives.

Family

Our greatest joy is associated with successfully starting a new relationship. This is true whether it is measured in terms of just the individual effect or in terms of the prevalence, and thus the aggregate impact; such is the joy of finding someone special. Hopefully, at least two people are made happier when this happens. Usually, of course, more people share in the happiness as well. Wider family and friends tend to approve, on average, of a new relationship beginning among their acquaintances.

The joy associated with starting a new relationship worthy of reporting at the end of a survey is, on balance, so great that people's reporting of their children finding love is a significant and positive event in their own lives, although it is four times less important to them in securing greater happiness as is finding someone for themselves: 4.32 times (0.160 divided by 0.037) according to the table in chapter 2. Statistics can be used to dull the most romantic of truths!

Making, keeping and not breaking relationships is more important than anything else to us humans. We are wired to worry about each other, to care for each other and to need to be cared for. Some suspect that the minority who are less attuned to the social are the ones who try hardest to argue that money is more important today.[109] As far as we can tell, from a long series of small studies, people with a huge amount of money are no better at maintaining happy relationships than people who have less, and they are possibly worse at it.[110]

If you accept that relationships are so important, what would you then want of a government, and of each other? Not seeing our relationships end prematurely through ill health turns out to be the most important need. But we have covered death and illness above. What we need is an understanding about how other government policies can help us stay together when we want to do so. Government can also make that harder in all kinds of ways.

It is easy to list all the things that governments do to separate people from their loved ones. An obvious one is to imprison them. The punishment of prison is the punishment of separation, and this is discussed in the next section. Governments can make it harder for people to stay housed, to keep to one job, to start a family, to avoid long commutes, to avoid having to move home frequently, and harder to avoid working excessive hours. In all these ways governments make it easier for us not to meet people, and more likely that we will split up.

Out of thirty-four countries with comparable data, the UK has the fourth highest annual divorce rate. Only in the US, Puerto Rico and Russia is divorce more common.[111] Countries where fewer people get married in the first place or where divorce is more difficult to obtain have lower rates, but even taking this into account the UK rate is remarkably high. Of course many couples in the UK never marry, but cohabiting relationships are no more secure than marriages. And we do know that the number of children brought up by one parent in the UK is high by international standards. Furthermore, the strain of poverty, inequality and poor housing makes sustaining relationships more difficult, and can help trigger domestic violence; and then, in turn, the children who witness domestic violence are more likely to commit crime and end up in prison later in life. At least 40% of those convicted of a crime and imprisoned have witnessed domestic violence at some point during their childhood.[112] All social issues are interlinked.

People need space and time for relationships. Opportunities to interact are curtailed because our leisure time and social interactions are cut when our working and commuting hours rise. Government can help ensure we have more leisure time. Policies such as six-hour days or more choice in general over when and whether to work (discussed later in this book) have implications for the health of our relationships. People need more time and space to both start and sustain a relationship, but also to be free to end it when it really has failed. Politics can help in all of this, as it did in the past when divorce laws were liberalized and, more recently, when same-sex marriage was legalized.

Prisons

The ultimate sanction government has, in a country without the death penalty, is to imprison people, breaking their relationships with others.

Prisons used to be small private affairs, locally organized, few and far between. Then they grew greatly in number and size during the Victorian period, with industrialization and urbanization. In the UK we imprison more people per capita than any other country in Europe. Women are disproportionately more likely than men to be imprisoned for non-violent offences, but men are far more likely to be in prison than women, especially men who grow up in poverty. As Michael Gove, the government's Secretary of State for Justice, put it in October 2015:

> Prisons were the 'biggest failure' in the criminal justice process. They failed to rehabilitate those caught behind their walls, and created a perpetual revolving door of release and reconviction.[113]

Around 7% of all children in the UK have had a parent imprisoned while they were growing up. This is not a small proportion and reflects just how many adults are incarcerated. It is the same proportion of the UK's children enrolled in private schools,[114] which is also very high for a European country. Very few children in most of the rest of Europe either attend a private school or have had a parent who has been imprisoned. The UK is the most divided of European societies.

We have so many prisons in the UK not because we are inherently particularly vindictive but because social relationships and safety nets have broken down over recent decades, and there is now much more fear of crime.[115] However, the most recent increase in the prison population in the UK has occurred with very little evidence of an overall increase in crime. Our judicial system may be becoming more vindictive.[116] Despite little overall rise in crime there has been an 18% increase in (mostly racist) hate crimes in the UK, rising from 44,471 recorded in 2013–14 to 52,528 in 2014–15.[117]

Fear is constantly used to defend both our rates of imprisonment and many more laudable but only palliative interventions.[118] In the summer of 2015 officials working for Kids Company, the now-defunct charity, claimed that without their charity workers, London would descend into savagery, arson and riot.[119] It was fear of yet more riots that led magistrates to impose such long prison sentences on people convicted of very minor offences during the 2011 riots in London and elsewhere. An unhappy, unequal, segregated and dysfunctional society is also a society that has more rioting, insurrection and theft.[120]

Prisons are the extreme example of the many ways in which current government policies harm our relationships with each other, and we already have more prison cells per head than any other country in Europe.[121] Despite the Secretary of State for Justice's recent lament about prison not working, the current government is planning a new large-scale, profit-making, private-sec-tor-led prison-building programme. Criminologists, and former chief constables, explain:

> At their very centre, prisons are unhealthy and dam-aging places for both prisoners and prison officers.... If we need fewer police and more social workers then government should plan for that. Such an approach could lead to a radical downsizing of the prison estate with the closure of old prisons and no need to build replacements.[122]

The government should stop relying on charities to rehabilitate prisoners. The UK should have a policy target to reduce prisoner numbers each year, as part of the politics of kindness.[123] We need to realize that some government policies actively break up the relationships that matter most to people. Most people see mass imprisonment as necessary to maintain law and order, but the long-term effect is more lawlessness and less order.

The 7% of our children who leave school with a parent having been imprisoned need far more of our resources than the children of the most affluent who are educated away from the rest of society and at such great expense. We need to create a society that sepa-rates us from each other far less than the one we now live in.

Anxiety

When we feel less valued, less loved and less secure, we become more anxious. Between 1993 and 2007 the number of people experiencing an anxiety-related mental health disorder in the UK rose by more than an eighth. An extra 800,000 people a year were diagnosed as suffering from an anxiety disorder in 2007 compared with 1993. At the extreme, over 6,000 people a year commit suicide (see chapter 2). Suicide is the leading single cause of death among men in the UK between the ages of twenty-five and forty-nine. And since these figures were collected – since the economic crash – the situation has become worse.[124] But suicide is just the tip of an iceberg of anxiety.

How do people in the UK deal with anxiety? We have 50,000 family doctors to help us – but at the same time we have 280,000 professionally qualified account-ants.[125] This is possibly the highest per capita number of accountants on the planet. Do we really need to train so many of them and have so few young people training in medicine, in nursing, in teaching or in social work?

In the UK, as Prem Sikka, professor of accounting at the University of Essex explains:

> If anything, accounting firms have undermined na-tional tax revenues and used their expertise to excel at money laundering, bribery, corruption and other antisocial practices.[126]

Why do we encourage so many of our apparently most talented young adults to go into careers in the financial services and consulting industries? Commentators often retort that if we took the City of London out of the UK economy, this would have a massive negative effect on Britain's ability to pay for social services and the NHS. However, other Western European countries, which are less reliant on their financiers for their tax base, fund their health services and social services better than we do in the UK.

Perhaps accountancy makes some people happy. As Mary Poppins sings sarcastically in 'A British Bank': 'When gazing at a graph that shows the profits up, their little cup of joy should overflow!'[127]

Countries that are very economically unequal end up with fewer carers and more bean-counters. As trust reduces, we begin to employ more and more people to audit others. The US has more lawyers per head than any other country, and those lawyers are most frequently found in the most unequal cities in the country, such as Miami and New Orleans.[128] An untrusting country has more crime and uses more lawyers in its everyday business, and routinely in the media, for fear of counter-litigation. Bosses in Britain 'seek a legal opinion' about their actions, and pay a lawyer, more often than in other European countries. Evidence is currently being amassed that suggests that it might well be a lack of moral values among our elite that is one of the key reasons why we have so many lawyers. The evidence collection tends to concentrate on why the US is so unusual in this regard, but it often includes the UK as a similar example.[129]

It is not just accountants, bankers and lawyers that are growing in number. In recent decades there have also been huge increases in the number of security guards being employed. We have more doorkeepers and private patrols because we now think we have to ensure our own and our property's safety more, because we have become more anxious. And the more economically divided we become, the more anxious we get and the less we trust others. In some parts of very affluent central London, the 2011 census revealed that the most prevalent occupation was being employed in security as a doorman and housed in dormitories nearby or in accommodation on the premises. People who lived locally were living in properties not as tenants but as 'guardians', protecting the property by being there, but having no legal right as tenants.[130] We know where the fear is most concentrated. So where is the love?

Levels of anxiety in the UK are high, and trust is low, as economist Avner Offer and epidemiologists Kate Pickett and Richard Wilkinson have explained to widespread acclaim. As a result, far more people in the UK are employed to look after the security of property and of financial assets than in all other affluent countries, aside from the US. Yet with fewer doctors available to the public, and numbers of nurses being low, to achieve minimal levels of cover, more nurses and doctors are now having to be employed on a temporary basis than ever before.[131]

We are consuming more and more antidepressants. We are seeing levels of anxiety rising in our younger people, especially among girls around the age of fifteen. People are more concerned about the future: about their own futures, about the future of their children, and then, when they think more widely than that, about what will happen to their neighbourhoods, cities and societies if we carry on with the politics we have.[132] Looking further afield, their worries become international: about immigration, about climate change, terrorism and the rising international gulf between the mega-rich and the mostly-poor.[133] We need to wean ourselves off our excessive preoccupation with finance; we should pay more attention to measuring 'happiness preservation' than to maximizing wealth. Higher government (collective) aspirations would have far-reaching implications, including for our well-being and for the security of our relationships.

Chapter 5

Esteem

> We're seeing the spontaneous rise of collaborative pro-
> duction: goods, services and organisations are appear-
> ing that no longer respond to the dictates of the market
> and the managerial hierarchy.
>
> — *Paul Mason*[134]

The second most important aspect of our lives in terms of making us happy is work. Here, our happiness rises not so much as a result of how much we are paid, but rather from whether we have a job at all and how secure it is.

Being paid well is very important. We show how much we disrespect people when we pay them a minimum wage rather than, at the very least, a living wage. However, just having a job is the most important thing when it comes to happiness and employment; then – after securing employment – being respected at work matters. Being shown that you are valued is important, but this finding also shows how much the formal labour market has come to dominate our thinking.

Roles that are not formally remunerated have come to count for less.

To various degrees the work of rearing babies, caring for children and most work involved in looking after the ill, the less able and the old has been ignored for a very long time. Household work, care within families and child rearing have been 'invisible' to economists for generation after generation, even though the people who do this work are among the biggest contributors to the economy. Such work makes it possible for others to take paid work. If people were to stop doing it, our economies would collapse under the pressure. If we all tried to pay one another (in a market) to do each other's housework, healthcare, old-age care and childcare, we would run out of money to do so, because the transaction costs would be too high. Some also argue that if states were brave and visionary, they would consider paying a wage and, later on, pensions to people who do these jobs on behalf of their families. This might be one way in which basic income could be introduced; but more on basic income shortly.

By the accounting of happiness economics, after dealing with your relationship ending, and then the death, or very poor health, of those near and dear to you, losing your job is most likely to make you unhappy. Gaining a job is the second best event that occurs to most people, but it is not associated with as much extra happiness as losing a job is associated with unhappiness and despair.

Jobs

We saw that with relationships it is better to have never loved at all than to have loved and lost. Alfred, Lord Tennyson was wrong when he suggested otherwise![135] The message is not dissimilar where employment is concerned. It is better to never have been in formal employment (which was the case for many women in the not too distant past) than to have been in and out of work repeatedly – especially at older ages; however, gaining another post after having lost one is a great joy, or at least a relief. Changing a job also tends to be associated with more happiness, but less than half as much as gaining one in the first place.

In the UK you receive significant compensation upon being made redundant only if you have been in steady employment for a long time, and even then only if your employer has a policy to pay more than the legal minimum. Now that work has become more precarious and short term, significant redundancy payments have become rarer. It is possible to have more stable work than we have now and to have unemployment benefits (as people in many other European countries have) that replace a large proportion of your salary for the first two years in which you might be searching for another job if you are made unemployed.

In traditional economics there is a great deal of literature that says that making unemployment and welfare benefits more generous reduces the incentives to find work. But, of course, it only reduces the incentives to find work you would not want to do. Increasing unemployment benefits does not decrease the incentive to work, when the incentive is not fear and desperation. In a well-functioning labour market employees are able to choose between jobs and to choose not to do jobs that are either too lowly paid or too uninteresting to them. Such a labour market has near full employment. In 2015 the lowest unemployment rate in the affluent world was 3.5% in Norway, followed by 4.0% in Japan and 4.2% in Switzerland – the figure for the UK was 7.2%.[136] Fortunately, there is a long list of influential economists who disagree with the traditional ways of thinking. For instance, consult Molly Scott Cato's work on green economics,[137] or Mariana Mazzucato's on entrepreneurial public spending,[138] or Kate Raworth's on the role of social justice in economics.[139]

People are most productive when they enjoy their work and are not being asked to work excessive hours. An experiment currently being undertaken in Sweden is described below. It is designed to try to work out whether, to increase productivity, it is better if full-time work is six hours a day rather than eight. New ways of working are currently emerging that allow people to work more flexibly. We have to work out how such flexibility doesn't also increase precariousness.

In living memory in Britain there was very little unemployment, and a genuine labour market where most people had some choice over what work they did. They did not much fear being labelled as redundant, or being disposed of as part of an 'efficiency drive'. There were also times, in the 1930s and 1880s, when we experienced mass unemployment and thought we might never return to having useful work for all. Given how important work is to us in the grand scheme of things, it is worth asking how we can ensure that the fate of our children and grandchildren is not as dependent on luck and timing as ours has been. If you are very successful, you have almost certainly also been very lucky.

Over the course of the past forty years, those in the highest-paid tenth of occupations have pulled ever further ahead.[140] Incomes have fallen at the bottom when compared with the rising cost of living. However, the living standards of nine out of ten of the best-off tenth have fallen since the 2008 crash. Only those who have secured a place in the best-off tenth of that 10% group – the 1% – have seen their real incomes increase since 2008.[141]

Within just the top 1%, it is again mostly those at the very top, in the top 0.1% of society, who have gained the most, but even they have gained less than the even richer 0.01%, even in relative terms! The lives of the super-rich are shrouded in secrecy, but when the details are revealed, often through divorce courts, the extremely wealthy and powerful tend not to have lives of unbridled happiness.

In January 2015 the apparent needs of a few to gain yet more esteem reached new heights of ridiculousness and tragedy. Some 1,700 private flights were scheduled by global business leaders to land at Zurich and other airports near to Davos so that the richest businessmen on the planet (and a tiny number of women) could meet and feel important and discuss the future of the planet, and threats such as climate change owing to carbon pollution. Even sharing a private jet with others racked up an individual return flight bill of £18,500, and the burning of more fuel in one hour than a car uses in a year.[142]

In the closeted world they occupy, global business leaders do not consider taking private flights excessive, because for them and their contemporaries it is normal. Waiting and being patient is, for them, not normal. Just as most of us would find it hard to travel by horse and cart today, they find it hard to travel as we travel. One great problem with esteem and employment is that there are so many different conceptions of normal nowadays. It is natural to think that how you behave is normal if you only compare yourself with those you consider to be your peers. But a better politics requires us all to have a wider understanding of normality.

You could argue that television and the Internet have massively opened peoples' eyes to different worlds, but these are often manufactured worlds. Parts of the media have created the cult of the celebrity, idolized the wealth and lifestyles of the super-rich, and manufactured poverty-porn for mass consumption. Other parts are more responsible and less puerile. Before them, the invention of the novel offered a window onto the lives of different groups in society and opened up peoples' eyes to how Britain's well-to-do lived (Jane Austen) and how its poor got by (Charles Dickens). People have always mainly set their view of normality by how their peers are faring, and what their priests and leaders tell them, but in recent generations a wider media has emerged and we can be better informed. Today we can gain a far better idea of notions of global sustainability, of equity and fairness, should we wish to.

Often what you can find out about the very well off is surprising. For instance, even in extremely equitable Sweden, just 3% of the population consume a quarter of all international flights by distance a year. In less equitable France, just 5% of the people fly half of all the air miles flown by the entire French population each year. [143] And, it turns out, such frequent and apparently exotic travel doesn't even much benefit the travellers. A government concerned with happiness would not expand airports.

Studies have found that among World Bank employees, those who were long-distance air commuters were three times more likely to suffer psychological illness. People who fly more get more disorientated, get less exercise and eat less well. They are exposed to a huge number of germs recycled in cabin air, to toxins in that air, to excess radiation due to altitude; they age faster, suffer deep-vein thrombosis more often, and, at the very least, suffer from repeated jet lag. Other studies also suggest that these 'hypermobile' individuals also tend not to have the happiest of home lives. [144] Being a high-flyer is not all it's made out to be.

At the top of the pay tree in the UK in 2015 was Sir Martin Sorrell, the chief executive of WPP, who received £43 million in that year: 3,486 times the minimum wage at the time. WPP is the world's largest marketing group, a firm that makes its money persuading people to buy things they would not otherwise want or bother to buy. Marketing has a similar effect on increasing consumption, and hence pollution, as unnecessarily frequent air travel. WPP has done very well for its clients, and so some £36 million of Sir Martin's pay packet was made up of long-term awards for what is called 'business success'. However, even the shareholders of the company, who also benefited from its growing profits, were angry about his 2015 level of remuneration.[145] Two weeks after Sir Martin's take was revealed, it was announced that Britain had become the most unequal country in Europe, according to an analysis of pay rates.[146]

In contrast to chief executive officers (CEOs), the lowest-paid workers in companies are rarely paid travel expenses (even if they drive between clients as care workers). The lowest paid in the UK also suffer much more from exhaustion and stress than their counterparts in more equitable countries. With the modest rise in the UK minimum wage in October 2015 to £6.70 an hour, some 390 minimum-wage workers can be employed for a year for the annual cost of the average CEO of a FTSE 100 company in the UK.[147]

Being paid 390 times less than someone else means that, in theory at least, you would have had to have started work in 1626 to be paid as much (by 2016) as they would have been paid in one year alone. King Charles I would have been crowned as you began your working life. After 100 years of labour you could have read *Gulliver's Travels*, Jonathan Swift's satirical account of inequality and society, published in 1726. After a further century of work you would have begun to see the dawn of industrialization in 1826. Another century on and you

The trickle-down effect

could have taken part in the General Strike of 1926. And finally, by 2016, you could have earned, and maybe even saved, as much as the boss of your firm might get paid in a year – if we forget your housing costs, food costs and the small problem of living that long. Oh, and you will have done all that as a woman, because the majority of people on the minimum wage are women, and women are still paid much less than men for doing the same work.

No doubt Sir Martin Sorrell has his own inspiring story to justify his high income. He has been paid far more than most of those CEOs. Almost everyone tells themselves stories that justify most of their actions, but, as psychologists Carol Tavris and Elliot Aronson explain, we all:

> need a few trusted naysayers in our lives, critics who are willing to puncture our protective bubble of self-justifications and yank us back to reality if we veer too far off. This is especially important for people in positions of power.[148]

Pay inequality in the public sector is far lower than in the private sector, and it is now also coming down in many cases. Table 3 uses data released by the National Audit Office in 2015. It shows the ratio of top pay to median pay in a number of selected organizations. Not all seventeen major government departments have released their pay ratios. Those that have failed to do so include the Department of Health, where inequalities in civil servant pay may

Table 3. Pay ratios in selected government departments and agencies (2013–15).

Ratio	Maximum	Median	Organization
4.7:1	£182,000–£185,000	£38,919	HM Treasury 2013–14
5.6:1	£200,000–£205,000	£30,640	Environment Agency (EA)
6.3:1	£160,000–£165,000	£29,185	Environment, farming, rural (Defra)
7.9:1	£197,500	£25,261	DCLG: Planning Inspectorate (Admin)
8.7:1	£195,000–£200,000	£22,669	HMRC 2013–14
8.5:1	£200,000–£205,000	£23,805	HMRC 2014–15

Source: the 2014 report can be found at https://www.nao.org.uk/Collections/short-guides-to-dep artments/ and the 2015 report can be found at https://www.nao.org.uk/search/pi_area/short -guides/type/report/.

be very high. However, inequalities within one department measured at two points in time are falling – that department is HM Revenue and Customs itself.[149]

Paying people at the top excessive amounts of money is just one very obvious signal that there is much that is very wrong with the world of work in the UK. We simply have to compare ourselves with any other country in Europe to see that pay inequalities indicated as being normal in table 3 are not tolerated elsewhere.

HMRC was not made more efficient by paying the person in charge 8.7 times the remuneration of the median worker in that department in 2013–14. Will that median (middle-ranking) employee, a tax inspector, feel well rewarded and motivated on a salary that remains below £24,000 when inspecting the tax affairs of others who receive so much more? The National Audit Office calculation of the median only takes into account those that are directly employed: it does not include cleaners if they are subcontracted, or those very highly paid officials who used to ask for their pay to be made out to their company rather than to themselves. The latter practice is now being outlawed, but the subcontracting of cleaners at below the living wage is not yet outlawed. If it were, happiness would rise.

At an individual level, stopping the rising trend in inequality is only easy if you are an employer or trustee of an organization, a director or an executive. Even then it is not simple. Your colleagues may well object to any curtailing of pay at the top because of what they describe as 'market forces'. But look at what HMRC has done in the table above. Median pay rose by 5% between 2013–14 and 2014–15, while top pay rose by half as much in percentage terms. But this is still almost five times as much in absolute terms: a rise at the top of £5,000, compared with the £1,136 pay rise for those in the middle that can be calculated from the table above. Relative pay gaps can fall while absolute differentials still rise.

Before concerning themselves with narrowing pay ratios, the first thing anyone in charge of any half-decent organization should do is immediately pay the living wage. This is not the Chancellor of the Exchequer's proposed 'national living wage', but the one that is calculated every year by academics at the University of Loughborough. The real living wage is not some fanciful utopian ideal. It is determined with the support of the Joseph Rowntree Foundation and the food and confectionery giant Nestlé. An organization that cannot pay the living wage may be badly run in other ways. People heading such organizations are beginning to realize that others might come to that conclusion about their ability. Outside of London the real living wage is £8.25 an hour. It may be higher when you read this, as rents and other costs are still rising quickly.

If you do not have control over wages, or if you are reliant on benefits or a pension, then you have to lobby

97

and campaign. Several organizations do this and they all need help: see www.shareaction.org/justpay, www.equalitytrust.org.uk and www.cpag.org.uk among many others. The list of organizations paying the true living wage is now very long, and it is getting longer. In January 2015 Brent Borough Council became the first local authority in the UK to offer businesses in their area a reduction of £5,000 in their business rates if the business became a living wage employer.[150]

We all need to concern ourselves with why the UK pay gap is growing. Two brilliant websites that help in this task are www.paycompare.org.uk/pay-multiples and http://highpaycentre.org, with the former reporting on the current pay gaps within many public and private bodies. So far the only business to actually refuse to reveal their pay gap is Barclays Bank (but at least they now pay the real living wage). We need greater and greater scrutiny of minimal and maximal pay, and to ask why the gap between the two is not closing.

We can compare ourselves with other countries. In 2014 part of Swedish local government began an experiment to see what would happen if public sector employees worked only six hours a day but were paid as if they had worked eight hours. Private sector workers in the car industry in Gothenburg had already made this transition and found that it increased efficiency. There was criticism, but the mayor replied:

we've worked a long time on this, we've not planned it to be an election thing. These people are always against shortening hours.[151]

A year later, when initial results were positive, many private and public sectors bodies took it up. Swedes were to be paid for eight hours a day but only asked to work for six hours a day. This was not just a 33.3% pay rise: it was an attempt to ensure that no one works for too long at one thing, and if they do that they work better in those six hours. Other aspects of their lives also improve, including their relationships within their families. Freedom and happiness increase when people have more time to choose what they want to do. Most people will not simply choose to have a siesta, but if they do, that is their choice.

The news of this Swedish experiment showing initial signs of success was picked up worldwide. Often, newspapers commenting on it would also inform their readers that there were health benefits to working fewer hours for better pay because:

> Working between 41 to 48 hours gives workers a 10 per cent higher risk of stroke, which then jumps to a 27 per cent increased risk if working 49 to 54 hours.[152]

People don't just produce worse work and have skewed priorities when they work too much. One business commentator in the US concluded: 'So Sweden has it right, and the US should follow.'[153]

In the Netherlands a different experiment is being developed. In the Dutch city of Utrecht a basic income is to be introduced during 2016. A randomly chosen group of welfare recipients in Utrecht will receive around €900 a month, with no conditions attached. Another group will continue to be subject to the normal regulations. The project's manager succinctly describes the theory as follows: 'We think that more people will be a little bit happier and find a job anyway.'[154] That theory is based on decades of academic work suggesting that basic incomes for all are preferable to means-tested welfare. In which case, why has it never been introduced before? One argument is that it would be good for removing the poverty trap but expensive if not introduced at a very low level, and there may possibly be other adverse incentives. Another argument against introducing a basic income is that the rich do not want to pay the extra taxes that would fund it. However, it could be what even their own children need to break the cycle of having to take work they do not want to do simply because it pays well. In 2017 Finland will begin to experiment with an €800 a month basic income, to be introduced by their centre-right government.[155] The idea is winning support from across a wide range of political viewpoints.

The central idea of a basic income is that very few people abuse the welfare system, and if the welfare system is about ensuring everyone has enough to live on, why not just give everyone just enough without question?

As any basic income is below a level most people would want to live on, almost everyone continues to carry out paid work, and part of the taxation of that paid income goes towards allowing everyone to have a basic income. However, once a basic income is high enough, people are free to choose not to do inadequately paid work, or even better-paid work that they do not see a value in doing, and so the labour market begins to function properly: people can exercise choice. A basic income could be introduced at a very low level, say just £1,040 a year, £20 a week, and then slowly increased. Imagine if one were introduced across the European Union at, say, €1,500 a year. That money would go further in poorer parts of the EU than in richer countries, and it would reduce the need for people to move between areas as much as they presently do.

When you introduce a basic income you remove most of the assessments required in means-tested systems, and all income gets taxed, much more progressively than at present. High wealth would also need to be taxed to pay for a basic income, so such schemes are fiercely opposed by some of the very wealthy. But no one would have to do a job that they think is stupid, or too unpleas-ant to justify the reward being given – just to survive.

Changes in how we live, work and interact are under way without the need for experimentation to instigate them, although the introduction of a basic income would accelerate these new trends. Paul Mason gave some examples in a 2015 *Guardian* article:

We're seeing the spontaneous rise of collaborative production: goods, services and organisations are appearing that no longer respond to the dictates of the market and the managerial hierarchy. The biggest information product in the world – Wikipedia – is made by volunteers for free, abolishing the encyclopaedia business and depriving the advertising industry of an estimated $3bn a year in revenue. Almost unnoticed, in the niches and hollows of the market system, whole swaths of economic life are beginning to move to a different rhythm. Parallel currencies, time banks, cooperatives and self-managed spaces have proliferated, barely noticed by the economics profession, and often as a direct result of the shattering of the old structures in the post-2008 crisis.[156]

So much is changing so quickly when it comes to the subject of work that it is easy to miss the good news stories: the experiments with shorter working weeks and with paying a basic income, and the amazingly rapid growth in collaborative working worldwide.[157]

A better politics for a happier, healthier UK would see the introduction of a basic income: it would initially be at a very low level, but it would be universal.

To make the labour market work well, people need to have real choices in that market over what work they want to do, when to work and for how long. Any small steps towards making labour an efficient market, as well as being more competitive and open, should be welcome.

Unemployment

The official UK unemployment rate is low by international standards, although still roughly twice that in each of Switzerland, Norway and Japan. However, in comparison with other European countries there are many who are self-employed and might not have much actual work, as well as high numbers of employees on zero-hours contracts who may not be paid much or anything in some weeks. This, and the lack of pay bargaining power that results, means that people are not doing useful jobs they would have chosen to do in a well-functioning 'free' labour market. 'Low' UK unemployment means one in six young adults cannot find a job and are claiming benefits for that reason: three times the rate for all adults. If full-time students who are often also searching for a job to make ends meet are included, youth unemployment rates are higher still. From 1945 to 1975, only one in fifty adults, both young and old, were unemployed at any one time in most years.[158] We have had a better-functioning labour market before, although in many towns for most people the bulk of the work on offer was only in a few factories and was usually extremely monotonous and often damaging to health. However, fewer women were in paid work then, partly because an average full-time factory wage could support a household. More women had been in work before 1945, when average pay had been lower, and so many more worked as servants.

It is very important to realize that statistical tricks and low benefit levels can make official unemployment rates appear lower than they are. Between 2008 and 2015, 3 million people in the US who had been working left the labour market and didn't register as unemployed because benefits there are so low.[159] This resulted in the reported US unemployment rate falling to 5.1% and zealous politicians claiming that all was well in the land of the free.[160] In the UK it is proposed that from April 2017 onwards adults aged under twenty-two will no longer be eligible for housing benefit payments. This will force them to stay with their parents and they will be unable to claim unemployment benefit if someone in their family has a job, so one headline measure of the unemployment rate will again appear to fall. These policies were announced in July 2015, at the same time as a newly elected UK government proposed to abolish the Child Poverty Act of 2010, replacing it with a new Life Chances Act of 2015 that would concentrate solely on ensuring young people had what the government described as 'chances'. Officials would no longer have a duty to be concerned about poverty.[161] Just before Christmas 2015, child poverty in the UK was reported to have fallen by 3.7 million – but only because the Life Chances Act changed the definition of poverty; in reality, child poverty rose.[162]

Between 2010 and 2015 in the UK, some £18 billion a year was cut from welfare benefits, instead of raising taxes, when the banks had to be bailed out. More cuts are to come in the very near future: 'Total managed expenditure is due to fall from 40.9% of national income in 2014–15 to 36.5% in 2019–20.'[163] As early as 2014, the initial cuts were hitting working families on low incomes with children the hardest. They were already losing £1,650 a year in tax credits and other benefits. This is a group of people who were already poor before losing this extra £4.53 a day. The cuts were concentrated on the North of England, being 43% higher there per family than in the South.[164]

In the UK we have imported a media culture from the US that feeds the myth that everyone has a chance. From *The Apprentice* to *Dragons' Den*, the message is 'try hard enough and you can make it'. There are all kinds of TV and radio programmes on entrepreneurship, and endless competitions. Everything is a competition, even making a cake (*The Great British Bake Off*). The BBC, the second most lauded national collective treasure after the NHS, is happily playing along, instead of helping to promote a different narrative.

One argument that has been made is that the loss of welfare support will have resulted in more people looking for work and finding work. By 2015 this claim had been tested, and the conclusion was that there was no evidence to support such a claim. Instead, a huge amount of pain has been inflicted for no evident gain. Within the UK it is the poorest people in the poorest neighbourhoods in the poorest cities and regions who have suffered the most as public spending falls. More local shops shut as people have less and less money to spend locally. There is a very large multiplier effect of cutting the incomes of the poor, because the poor spend all their income.

Back in the 1990s people had little idea that in Britain, and much of the rest of the rich world, they were living in a period that would later be seen as the start of an economic boom that would turn to bust in 2008. The cartoon on the facing page is an updated version of a very famous cartoon that was popular in the 1930s. Back then the salary of the man at the top was £10,000 a year and he wore a top hat, the man below him lived on £1,000 a year and wore a bowler hat, the man below him wore a trilby, and the man at the bottom had a flat cap and was unemployed. Although the times have changed and it is now

a woman at the bottom, the concept remains the same. However, one difference between now and the 1930s is that the man at the top is stepping up a rung, not down. Economic inequality features repeatedly in the pages that follow, even though no one states in a survey that in the past year they noticed inequality rising and affecting their family. We have to link what people say matters to them with that which then affects those events the most.

The real rates of unemployment and underemployment are far higher than is revealed by official figures. Surveys that ask people if they would like work, or fulltime work, reveal that there are many more such people than those who are claiming benefits. Many people may disguise their unemployment through registering for tax purposes as self-employed, or simply by describing themselves as self-employed on a census form, when they actually have little or no work.

Disrespect

There is far more to enabling people to enjoy the esteem they could have than simply reducing pay inequalities and unemployment. For instance, groups that advocate better rights for women explain that a fairer society cannot be achieved through solely eradicating the gender pay gap, improving childcare and instituting other progressive measures. For example, even if all the Scandinavian countries' policies were adopted in the UK, this would not eliminate gender-based violence, which still remains high in Scandinavia but is also possibly better recorded there than in less-equal affluent societies.[165] All Western societies, even those in Scandinavia, remain patriarchal, including some other countries with low income inequality, such as Japan and South Korea.

A patriarchy is a society controlled by men. It may include many women. It tends to give much more weight to a particular old-fashioned set of economic concerns over and above social, environmental and more enlightened economic concerns. It tends to not be inclusive when considering policy and planning objectives. Patriarchy values individual needs over social connections. It sees productivity as being only about money, and not about the production of new human lives or the development of a society that is mutually supportive. Patriarchy does not see the public sector as a mitigating force when markets, to various degrees, fail. No sane family would arrange its internal dynamics using market forces. Although families are one of the mechanisms that reproduce and maintain broader social inequalities, families are also based on love.[166] Our love and caring for others need not be constrained to our now very small families.[167]

In the UK today the main roles for many women are often seen as the solution to care issues. The love and enjoyment involved in childcare and other care is routinely undervalued. Women are still routinely objectified as sexual objects in UK culture and in public discourse. We know the situation is in many ways much better than it was a generation ago, so we do not see how antiquated our current behaviour and social norms may appear in a generation's time – if there is more progress. Women in the UK are still the targets of systemic abuse and serious violence on a scale that may well be remarked upon in future as having been intolerable, but which is currently seen as normal. Institutionally, through gender inequalities, and individually, usually within families, women suffer far more abuse than men. Families may be based on love, but there is often a great deal of hate within them, and that in turn is influenced by the nature of the society within which families form, exist and try to sustain themselves.

The kinds of policies that are needed include free universal childcare for under-fives, including the option to care for your own children. Looking after your own young children should not be unaffordable. We should not pay people so badly that all adults in a family have to take paid work. Flexible working needs to be introduced across all businesses and all sectors, and this is a requirement that will soon become more urgent because of our ageing population. The disproportionate poverty rates for women need to be tackled. Two-thirds of those earning under £10,000 a year, and usually receiving much less than that, are women. One in four older women in the UK live below the poverty line.[168]

Trying to reduce gender inequalities today is like swimming against the tide of this decade. The UK government plans to try to remove feminism from the A-level politics syllabus in a move reminiscent of its earlier attempts to remove climate change from the study of geography in UK schools.[169] Aggregated household statistics ignore women's inequitable access to family income and lead to policy that often does not properly cater for women. The 2010–15 coalition government reduced tax bills by £17 billion, and 58% of the beneficiaries were men. Men arrange to pay themselves more than women.[170] Claiming that these reductions in tax will help the men's families demands a particularly quaint view of families.

Despite the legal acceptance of gay marriage, there is currently a discriminatory emphasis on the importance of the supposed traditional nuclear family, which can lead, among much else, to cases of violence against women being seen as unimportant. There are plans being executed now to bring in a form of universal credit and replace tax credits with higher tax allowances, in a way that is anticipated to adversely affect women much more than men.

Parliament should assess all economic decisions to determine whether they might adversely impact women's lives disproportionately and increase or lower economic inequalities more generally. Child benefit needs to be both restored as universal and raised in line with real earnings. Action is required on discrimination in the workplace, including pregnancy, maternity leave and pay discrimination, and support for childcare and part-time working needs to be improved.[171]

The position of women in British society is worsening now, but over recent decades it had been improving and beneath the surface it may still be improving in a way that will soon have beneficial effects that may come as something of a surprise. A new book by Dawn Foster called *Lean Out* was published in January 2016. It critiques Sheryl Sandberg's *Lean In*, a guide for women in business, explaining that for all the commercial success of a very small number of women, their success has been achieved by an approach that is individualistic and largely unthreatening to male-dominated capital.[172] Far more women than men now graduate from UK universities. Do we really think that such a highly educated new young cohort will not change the world for the better? Do you think that millions of female graduates (and male ones too) in the UK will in future teach their sons and daughters to be servile, or will they teach them to stand up to the few men controlling so much of our money? Half of all young women in England now go to university, and that recent shift in educational patterns could have a huge impact in the future. The next generation could be transformational.

Chapter 6

Education

> Education should indeed be responsive to the needs of society. But this is not the same as regarding yourself as a service station for neo-capitalism.
>
> — *Terry Eagleton*[173]

As people gain more education, they become more conscious of their own ability, have more scope to increase that ability, and feel more valued and recognised by others. Unlike sharing out land, housing and much other material wealth, education is not a zero-sum game. Everyone could feel more valued and be better educated without others needing to have less, but achieving this requires a better politics than we currently have.

Self-actualization appears in the upper reaches of Maslow's hierarchy. Education aids such actualization. Education in the UK should be more about learning to be creative and less about conforming to unimaginative syllabuses and passing exams.[174] The conformity created by exam results and school league tables will also disempower young people in the future world of work, as another wave of automation changes the future skills that are going to be most needed in future employment.

School

After starting a new relationship, acquiring a job, securing a home and becoming a parent or grandparent, the next most important event associated with gaining more happiness is doing well in education. Sadly, when people comment on their children's educational achievements over the past year, they often register disappointment. Table 1 in chapter 2 shows that parents are more unhappy than usual when they comment on their children's education, in contrast to young adults, who talk more positively about educational experiences. More UK parents seem upset with how their children are doing at school than are impressed.

There are particular aspects of the British education system that are unusual compared with otherwise similar countries. In 2013–14, the most recent year for which there is data for England, the number of children who were permanently excluded from primary schools included some 6,510 children with Special Educational Needs and Disability (SEND) statements. In addition, a further 30,230 children with SEND but no statement (i.e. those that did not require special provision) and a further 8,280 children who were not labelled as SEND were also permanently excluded. It is possible that more children are permanently excluded from primary schools in the UK each year than are expelled from all the other primary schools of Europe combined.

For secondary schools, most students who are permanently excluded are those with special needs or disabilities. In 2013–14 in England alone these included some 13,340 secondary-aged children with SEND statements and 96,750 with SEND but no statement (a further 100,490 were excluded without being labelled as SEND).

These numbers are enormous.[175] We simply do not know what happens to all the excluded children. Such high rates of school exclusion make little sense in terms of the wider effects on everyone outside of the school.

For children expelled from inner London state schools at the age of ten, the average cost per child to the state of dealing with the consequences in the subsequent eighteen years was £70,019 according to a study published in the *British Medical Journal* in 2001 that has withstood any revision since then.[176] This is the average cost of subsequent criminal damage, drug dependency and treatment after subtracting the normal incidence of those things. But in the short term it makes the school's statistics look better. The school has a strong incentive to opt for exclusion because it will help its closely monitored results data. How can we be excluding so many ten-year-olds in England and not asking, in shock, why we do this to such young children?

In most of the rest of Europe children do not go to school quite as early as they do in the UK, and children are not tested at the age of four or five, when they arrive, as they currently are in England. Those tests have been shown to be extremely unreliable and potentially very harmful for children and schools.[177]

In 2008, 30.5% of all educational expenditure in the UK was private, mostly on the 7% of children who attend private schools. On average, between four and five times as much is spent on each privately educated child per year as is spent on each state-educated child's provision.[178] The next highest private education spending in Europe was in Cyprus, where 17.3% of education spending goes on a small minority. In contrast, private education spending is lowest in Norway (1.8%), Finland (2.6%) and Sweden (2.7%). This spending includes monies spent on home tutors, pre-school education and tuition fees, so in these three countries, and in most of the rest of mainland Europe, there is hardly any private school education. Overall, state spending on education in the UK per child is lower than in many other European countries. This is not surprising, as when most of the elite who control national budgets do not use state education for their own children, why would they care much about low rates of spending in state schools?

If this system were beneficial, the UK would not be languishing, as it is, at the bottom of several education league tables when the richest twenty-five large countries of the world are compared.[179] Within the UK, Scotland and Wales have universal comprehensive education, while Northern Ireland still has widespread class (grammar school) and religious (sectarian) school segregation. The current education system does not benefit the affluent English very much, however, as they become even more out of touch and segregated, and are trained to pass exams rather than learn.[180]

The UK does very badly in international comparisons when young adults are examined at ages up to twenty-four. Repeated examining means that in England and Wales we learn for the day of the test and not in a way that helps us retain what we were taught, nor are we taught how to approach problems imaginatively, so we do badly when tested again at ages up to and including twenty-four.[181] Although there are variations around the UK, all four devolved nations test children repeatedly and use these tests to rank children according to 'ability' or 'potential'. Very many go on to universities later, with their own hierarchies of reputation, and then to different kinds of job with huge ranges of income and status. It is possible that no other country in the world has as great a range of university scores in international league tables as the range in the UK.

The British tolerance of extreme differences can hurt those at the top as well as those at the bottom. While it is true that most children in private schools do not board[182] and that they achieve very high exam grades on average (and higher pay later), they have been trained in a particular way, taking examinations very seriously at the expense of other ways of developing the ability to learn. And does Britain as a whole benefit from being led so disproportionately by people who have had such narrow training to jump through particular examination hoops, rather than a more well-rounded education during which they mixed with a cross-section of all in society?

Inclusion, respect and working together are not qualities that have been in vogue in English education in recent years. A leading educationalist, Sally Tomlinson, put it succinctly in 2015: 'the neo-liberal dream of competitive individualism now guides educational consciousness and sensibility'.[183] And this affects the privileged as much as the underprivileged. Carry on this way and every child has to compete harder than the children before them, each must learn to perform better to the test, and control and constrain their imaginations more than those before them did. Our schools risk looking and becoming more and more like exam factories.

Reports are produced each year on the biases involved in the recruitment of people to jobs in the UK. The small minority of university graduates who have been to private schools take up the large majority of starter jobs in elite financial firms and legal firms in the City of London. Those who recruit for these jobs know full well about this bias but respond: 'How much mud do I have to sift through in that [state-educated] population to find that diamond?'[184] The study that led to that comment being made explained that it had now become necessary 'to challenge dominant narratives which circulate within the professions about the meaning of merit/talent'.[185]

The increasing dominance of private schools in UK public life is a common complaint. It is not just that people with private school backgrounds dominate in law, politics, journalism and the upper echelons of management,[186] it is that they now dominate even in drama, on TV and in sport at the elite Olympic level,[187] and even in 'popular culture'. According a 2010 column in *The Word*, 'around 60% of chart pop and rock acts came from a private school background, whereas twenty years earlier it had been closer to 1%'.[188] That statistic turned out to be something of an exaggeration, but the original writer of the article has later explained that:

> poshification of pop is, I maintain, a reality. And that growing stranglehold is as bad for pop as it is for society.[189]

A survey of 2,500 people working in the arts that was released in late 2015 confirmed that 75% had had a parent able to support them so they could work for free to get into that business.[190] In such a climate, someone who does not quickly achieve great things, or at the very least a high salary, despite belonging to the 7% who are privately educated can easily come to feel inadequate.

The inequality within the education system fosters separation and fear. A few of us struggle to pay for our children to go to the most expensive schools we can afford, and more of us try to afford to live in the catchment area of what we consider to be a good school. We may then give our children the impression that for us not to achieve this would have been a terrible fate, and that they should copy our choices when they are adults. Our children have little understanding of other children's lives, of other options, because they mix only with children in the same narrow band of the hierarchy.

So segregated have we become that we start treating different groups of people almost as different species. Large sections of the population are demonized as 'chavs'.[191] It is in this context that schools, especially those in England, have to try to teach.

We have socially engineered the current situation and it makes people callous. It makes some claim that they would work less hard if they had to give 50% of any extra income to the government, rather than continue to pay tax at 45% over a certain, very high, salary level. Those same people then often suggest that there is another type of person who should be content to work more hours for a quarter of the minimum wage – which is what the introduction of universal credit, as currently planned, would do with a 75% 'taper rate'.[192] The idea that such behaviour is reasonable has been created by our current social and educational systems.

We need to recognize that our competitive schooling system in the UK produces poor results by international standards. Better policy options would look more often to schools in other countries. Our children are not well served by how we organize our schools, our examinations and our society. This applies to the most supposedly privileged child, segregated at an early age away from others, as much as it applies to the rest of us. Without a better framework for our education system, most of the inequalities covered in this book will continue to be socially reproduced and will perpetuate.

Universities

Children from state schools, on average, do a little better at university than children from private schools in terms of the likelihood of gaining a 2:1 or a first-class degree. One of the reasons for this may simply be because they went to a state school. State school pupils find university study easier – and they find being in an environment with a wide mix of other people easier too. There are many advantages to non-selective state schools.[193] The fact that they are the high achievers from within their state schools explains only five of the nine-percentage-point advantage that state school children with the same A-level grades have at university.[194]

Despite their disadvantages, even privately educated children who do poorly at university proceed, on average, to earn more than those who did better than them at school and university but who were not from such affluent families.

The findings just outlined do not mean that state-schooled children do well in general. Some economists have called for increased downward mobility of those from affluent backgrounds and schooling, to make room for upward mobility.[195] This is tantamount to a call for yet more competition and angst amongst the rich to match that existing among the poor. It is no child's fault if they attended a private or selective state school. Their parents are almost always simply trying to do the best for them. A solution to all this angst to get your child to the top would be to work towards achieving much smaller income gaps between all occupations, and also towards reducing the income gap between those not working and those in employment. If higher incomes were not so high, if top jobs were not perched on such a steep and slippery slope, everyone would benefit.[196]

Another case that now needs to be better made in the UK is the argument for higher education to be free at the point of delivery and paid for by all, not individually or by family. You would not ask adults to choose what level of healthcare they might want in future and then suggest they take out a loan to pay for it, so why do the same in university education? Yet we now have high university tuition fees in England. In most of Europe, and much of the rest of the UK, there are no, or low, university fees.

Current university students, future students, those already paying back fees and the parents and grandparents of all these groups know that many of the tuition and maintenance loans will never be repaid. At least they would know that if they looked carefully at the terms and conditions of the student loan. Although most graduates will never fully repay their loan, they will be paying out a great deal of their future earnings in interest payments. Their university education will cost them very dear in future. And they also need to be aware that those terms and conditions can be arbitrarily and retrospectively changed at any point, with no consultation, in order to increase payments in the short term (as happened in autumn 2015). Future taxpayers will have to make up any shortfall, which will include that same cohort who are now young graduates. One reason many leading members of the London-based establishment still favour loans is that they themselves are wealthy enough to pay their children's university fees upfront.[197]

Nick Hillman has helpfully written a small booklet that shows that the UK is very similar to Germany – indeed his publication is so clear that, although he has argued the opposite, it demonstrates that we could run their system instead of our own.[198] A large part of a better politics involves unravelling mistakes made in our recent past. They might not have originally looked like mistakes, because in the past higher education was so dominated by the upper middle class that public funding of it appeared to be a subsidy to the affluent, but that funding was withdrawn just at the time when more and more working class children, especially women, started to get into universities. There is a deep irony in the timing of the decision over the largest absolute rise in loans to £9,000 in 2010. In that same year it was announced that, for the first time, a majority of young women in England were going to university: 51%. This contrasts with a figure of less than 40% for young men.[199] Many, if not most, of those women will never earn as much as an average non-graduate plumber or taxi driver, let alone the even higher paid men, but they will still have to spend years paying the interest on the loans they were encouraged to think of taking out when they were still children.

Germans still value the role of higher education and high-quality technical education. People in Germany pay more in tax and less in rent. UK governments continue to make the argument that:

> At current tax levels, governments can no longer afford to be the primary or nearly sole source of revenues for public higher education, and market-related solutions seem inevitable.[200]

Of course, one alternative would be to tax income at levels similar to those in Germany, and then, suddenly, the inevitable would become entirely avoidable.

We should learn what not to do by looking at the US, where the lowest-paid university lecturers have seen a real-terms pay cut of 20% between 1986 and 2015, in spite of rising fees – fees that were instead used to triple the pay of state-funded college presidents. It is also notable that US student fees have risen dramatically, while the number of individuals employed in US universities earning a million dollars a year has doubled.[201] This simply does not happen in other countries that do not have such high student fees – which is most other affluent countries worldwide.

In the US most universities are still officially non-profit organizations, but some are now profit making. Look at the attempts in the US in 2014 to pass bills in the Senate to refinance student loans at lower interest rates; to refinance the loans again in 2015 through the failed Student Loan Relief Act; and now the serious proposals by one of the two main Democratic nominees to stand for president to make public college education free.[202] In late 2015 retrospective changes were made to the terms of UK student loans. These brought forward the point at which they must be repaid. The repayment scheme that had been promised when the loans were taken out was revised for students already at university. Children who decided to go to university on the basis of one loan scheme found it altered once they were studying at university. Why should anyone believe a government that misleads children like this?

A university system based on loans is unsustainable in the medium term. In the short term it has resulted in the sector being at least a billion pounds better off than it was a few years ago, but the cost of that extra borrowing to people who are currently aged eighteen to twenty-one will be far more than a billion pounds. By 2020, eight years' worth of English students and graduates will be carrying the highest student loan debt in Europe. Most of these new young debtors will be young women.

Education and the environment

Education should not be about getting into so much debt, competing so hard for grades or being misled so much by adults. It should be about learning, growing and enjoying studying – and it was in our recent past. The survey (again see table 1 in chapter 2) suggests that education and leisure activities both increase happiness, almost identically: they are the sixth and seventh most significant life events. Travelling for leisure is associated with happiness, and we typically learn more when we travel. However, the way we live and spend our leisure time impacts upon our environment, which in turn affects us. Travel uses energy and can add to pollution through greenhouse gas emissions.

Despite climate change being so high on the global agenda, and such an important part of so much of our recent education, research and learning, the UK government is currently cutting back most of the support that had been put in place to enable green energy providers to grow.[203] In just a couple of days in autumn 2015, two solar energy firms went bust with the loss of 20,000 jobs because of a change in UK government policy. The editorial of the *Observer* newspaper responded:

> Just another in a long line of changes that have hit energy efficiency, onshore wind, biomass and many other sectors that create jobs and a lower-carbon economy. These cuts looked particularly irresponsible in the run-up to the UN climate change talks in Paris, but at any time it is odd to see a party that wants to make Britain greater showing little time for nurturing a new business sector.[205]

Our inability to respond well to climate change is a good example of how we have not been learning.

A shift from long-distance travel to more local travel would reduce the environmental cost – and there is often a lot to explore close to home. Our cities could be so much better arranged to make travel within them, and between them, easier and greener. We could spread out our museums, galleries, concert halls and exhibition spaces so much better across the country. Almost all major public arts spending in the UK is concentrated in London. We need to learn both how to travel better and to consume less. In more economically equitable countries public transport tends to be of higher quality, fewer people drive (why do we in the UK love cars so much?) and housing is more often located close to the industry and services where people work. In these countries neighbourhoods are more socially mixed and social mixing is easier because the economic gaps between rich and poor are narrower.

It seems that buying a car does make people happy. Men buy more cars than women do and drive cars more often, especially at older ages. Why does the purchase of a car make men in the UK happier? And how do British men compare with those in Japan, where a car is only a necessity in rural areas, or in the Netherlands, where over half the population walk or cycle to work? Have we in the UK really learned a great deal if we still value car ownership so highly?

It is not just that car ownership is valued too highly in the UK, or that an overly competitive education system makes us all less smart, or that our job market gives such high rewards to those at the top compared with those at the bottom, or that the accumulation of wealth is valued so greatly over the accumulation of belonging, loving and caring. We need to learn to value the environment we live in better, to value travel that inspires us over travelling fast. We need to learn to pollute less, teach children in better ways and examine them less. We have great expectations of our children. We hope that they will see things more clearly than we have and act better than we have; but previous generations have suddenly seen things much more clearly than before and acted on that insight. It is not impossible to see great change within just a single generation. As one long-dead economist once said, in his hopes for a future after capitalism:

> The love of money as a possession ... will be recognised for what it is, a somewhat disgusting morbidity, one of those semi-criminal, semi-pathological propensities, which one hands over with a shudder to specialists in mental disease.[206]

John Maynard Keynes, who died in 1946, also forecast that by 2030, a hundred years from when he was writing, our lives would be more leisure-filled, and we would be working on average only fifteen hours a week in paid work.[207] He forecast that we would all be happier. Yet many people in Britain now cannot afford an annual holiday. This includes almost half of all families with children.[208]

Chapter 7

Conclusion

> Insecurity has become pervasive. It permeates the lives
> not just of the marginalised but also the reasonably well
> off. Our lives feel beyond our control.
> — *Ruth Lister and Neil Lawson*[209]

Looking at how we govern ourselves from the
perspective of what most matters to us, things
appear in a very different light. It is not possible to give
everyone a large financial windfall, but we can all be
happier.

The government that came to power in 2010 in the
UK chose to try to spend a lower proportion of GDP on
the public good than almost any other government in
Europe, and was even forecast to spend less than the US.
It did not manage to do that, because debt repayments
were too high. But its successor government elected in
2015 aims to get close to being that internationally minimal public provider by 2020.

Figure 2 illustrates just how wide is the range of
choices that affluent countries make in terms of public

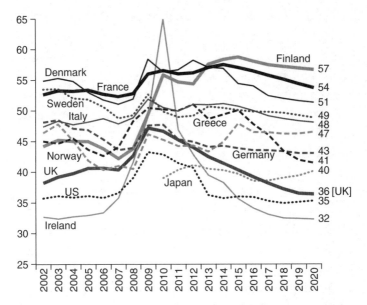

Figure 2. State spending as a proportion of GDP for twelve rich countries (2002–20).

Source: the 2010, 2012 and 2015 IMF databases, with projections after 2014.

spending levels, and that range is set to become wider still by 2020. Some countries choose to tax and spend more collectively rather than individually. These tend to be the more economically equitable countries, such as Finland, France and Denmark. In contrast, the more unequal English-speaking countries, including Ireland and the US, stand out as being (or becoming) the lowest taxers and spenders.

The graph is based on data from October 2015. According to these World Economic Outlook figures, produced annually by the IMF, Finland is projected to spend 57% of GDP on public services in 2020; France 54%; Denmark, Belgium and Austria will spend 51%; Sweden will spend 49%; Italy 48%; Portugal and Norway 47%; Germany 43%; the Netherlands 42%; Greece 41%; Japan 40%; and Canada and Spain each 39%. The latter two countries (not all are included in the graph as too many lines in the middle would then overlap) also spend more than the UK, or will do from 2016 onwards given planned cuts. After which UK public spending will be just 36% of GDP.

There is no guarantee that public spending is well directed. A great deal of public money is spent on arms, on inefficient officials and on vanity projects; but private spending can be at least as inefficient and vain – even dangerous. Vanity private projects can include purchasing second or third homes. In 1899 the economist Thorstein Veblen first identified the rise in vanity purchases among the rich, which only abated decades later. He called the new trend 'conspicuous consumption': spending to impress others.[210]

As I write (in February 2016) our government still aims to get spending down to 36% of GDP; a post-war and European low. What figure 2 demonstrates is that the UK is not a high-taxing, high-public-spending nation, although there is ample conspicuous private consumption.

The essence of the argument of this book is: do what will make most people happier and take more care to avoid causing harm. I am impressed by facts and figures. For example, instead of just 11% of working people being paid under the living wage (as one former MP recently incorrectly suggested was the case[211]), it turns out that by 2014 some 23% of all those people who were working outside London were paid so little; a pro-portion rising from 21% two years earlier. This is despite over 200 large firms having recently agreed to pay the living wage, including Barclays, RBS, Lidl and Ikea. Even with these recent commitments, huge numbers of UK workers are still paid less than £7.85 an hour – more than two-fifths of everyone in work in West Somerset, for example.[212] But there is at least some good news in that more and more people are actually being paid at this level.

More and more employers are being won round to believing that paying the living wage is the right action to take, and something they can do that is of worth. The social benefits of decent pay are significant, from reduc-ing money worries to increasing local spending. Try to imagine how many more large companies could and will commit to paying the real living wage soon. When will the first major hotel chain commit to it and become the brand of choice, especially for anyone spending public money on a hotel?

What follows are a few more ideas for practical steps that could be taken in the next few years.

We clearly need a reappraisal of our tax system. Far greater sums of money are raised by taxation in countries where tax is made fairer, the rich are less exempt and the income distribution is less dramatically skewed.[213]

Housing was discussed in chapter 3, and one conclusion to draw from the housing crisis is that we need to move towards taxing property wealth on an annual basis, which would require a reform of council tax. Such a move would allow both the abolition of income tax for the very low paid ('making work pay') and the introduction of a basic income for all (discussed in chapter 5), albeit initially at a very low level. This is a radical step that would require a change in our wider understanding of what is needed for an economy to work well. Higher wealth and, especially, property taxation would have the effect of damping down the housing market, but it would put more money into the real economy. An economy that was better balanced would raise employment in meaningful work. Wouldn't it be a good thing if fewer people worked as prison guards supervising a large section of the population (discussed in chapter 4), or as bankers sending money round in circles within the financial casino?

A green community energy revolution needs to be instigated, literally giving power to the people. This is already happening elsewhere in Europe, in towns like Freiberg, where trams are powered by electricity largely generated by local wind and solar sources, where so many people cycle and walk.[214] Getting there required a mixture of incentives, intervention, changes in the power of retail energy providers, changes in the planning process and pump priming. There are many nearby examples to study – if we wish to look.

We also need to concentrate on our immediate problems more, such as housing. Very few of us are actually homeless, but what of future generations? A building programme is needed. We could use the existing legislation that gave us the new towns of the 1960s and 1970s, but this time at least 250,000 (preferably carbon-neutral) homes need to be constructed over a four-year period, with integrated energy generation, public transport infrastructure, and possibly even food production. Along with new homes, built by councils or democratically constituted housing associations, we need new community structures, community buildings, public transport infrastructure, and workplaces. With fairer property taxation the uplift in the value of the land could be harnessed to make new building self-financing. The state is needed to ensure that any development is coordinated. Only the state – us, working collectively – can see the wider picture.

But what about the personal picture, such as issues concerning savings, which I first mentioned in chapter 3? Regional mutual banks for local people to save in and bank with, and for small local businesses to borrow from, could be encouraged. This would be possible if government had the courage to begin to reduce its underwriting of the largest four banks and to increase its underwriting of regional mutual banks. These regional institutions could also be encouraged to invest in high-tech low-carbon manufacturing in return for the government underwriting them.[215]

Of course there are some who think that all this talk of how much better things could be is fanciful. They think most people are fundamentally selfish, and that such selfishness can be tempered only a little.[216] In his book *How to Be a Conservative*, Roger Scruton uses the word 'truth' in eight of his chapter titles, so convinced is he that he knows what it is.[217] None of us can know for sure what proportion of what we suggest will turn out to be misguided and where we might have hit the nail on the head. That is often only apparent in retrospect.

But all of us can hope and dream and act and advocate. We can all look beyond our own shores to see if other people have made a better go of it than we have. We also need to be more suspicious of the motives of multinational corporations.[218]

We can also imagine children being automatically protected from poverty and debt by adequate universal child benefit and being given free care, and education from early childhood through to the end of university. This could be paid for by cuts elsewhere, and higher taxes, as is normal in the rest of Europe. Figure 2 showed how most affluent countries choose to tax and spend far more than we do, but it does not show that often they also spend that money better than we do in almost all areas other than healthcare. Our public health spending is still more efficient than in most other affluent countries, although its effectiveness is under threat.

Of the twelve affluent nations compared in figure 2, the UK is one of the very lowest in spending on health. Only Greece and Italy spend (slightly) less per person when private and state health spending are combined. Elsewhere in Europe health spending per person was twice as much in Switzerland as in the UK in 2013, and it was 81% higher in Norway, 59% higher in the Netherlands, 49% higher in Germany, 41% higher in Denmark, and 27% higher in France.[219] The UK commits less money per head than any comparable country to healthcare. People are beginning to notice this and ask why we can't have a better NHS.

So how do we change things before it is too late?

Vote; but before you can vote you have to be registered to vote. By mid 2015 it became clear that 1.9 million people who had been on the UK electoral roll under the old method of registering households were no longer listed. The old method allowed any person in a household to register everyone else living there. Many of the unregistered are very young adults. The number of unregistered voters is growing rapidly as private renting grows.[220] London alone will lose between six and eight constituencies in any redrawing of political boundaries as a result of that drop in registered voters.[221]

The referendum on independence in Scotland showed how many people, including sixteen- and seventeen-year-olds, would vote when presented with something they were passionate about. In the US, where huge numbers of people are imprisoned and unable to vote, recent research has shown that simply providing former prisoners with a small amount of information can increase by a huge proportion the likelihood of them both registering to vote and voting.[222] A third of the electorate did not vote in the May 2015 general election, and only a quarter of the UK electorate voted for the Conservative party that won. In 2005 it had been even worse, when just 20% of the electorate voted for the Labour Party and yet the party still won a majority of seats. No other rich country has an electoral system that can deliver such undemocratic results. We need a proportional voting system for Westminster elections, but the UK's two largest political parties have been opposed to fair votes when they have held power.

Until we get fairer votes we need to understand electoral geography and how informal political pacts work. In 2015 in the Sheffield Hallam constituency, the Conservative party hardly campaigned at all, giving their potential voters the message they should vote for Nick Clegg, then leader of the Liberal Democrats. They did not want Labour to win the seat if their voters voted Conservative. Clegg held his seat. At the same time, Labour won the City of Chester seat from the Conservatives when the Greens chose not to put up a candidate due to local concerns over fracking, of which the Conservatives were in favour. Labour won Chester with a majority of 93 – the smallest majority in the country, after three recounts.[223]

No tactical voting shenanigans will be necessary when the 'Westminster' UK parliament eventually has a fair voting system of the kind that is usual in the rest of the world, in European elections in the UK, and already in London, Scotland, Wales and Northern Ireland. Think a little further ahead and it is even possible to imagine the UK parliament not being in Westminster. When the Palace of Westminster has to undergo its ten-year renovation programme we could put parliament just to the east of Birmingham, where the two planned high-speed rail lines from the North East and North West are due to converge before heading to London.[224]

Something very new is happening in politics in the UK. It began in Scotland with the very close-run referendum result of 2014, and it is now reaching into England, where no one predicted Jeremy Corbyn would win so much support and be elected Labour leader in 2015 or that his party would win so many votes in the Oldham by-election later that year. It began earlier elsewhere in Europe when Green parties emerged as significant forces. It began on the streets of cities in the US in the form of new protests against the power of the 1% after evictions and bankruptcies rose so steeply following the 2008 crash. There is a new progressive politics growing worldwide, a yearning for greater equality and more stability.

However, at the same time, the populism of the far right has also risen again, as illustrated by the Tea Party in the US and the popularity of Donald Trump as the potential US Republican presidential candidate in early 2016, by the rising popularity of close-to-fascist parties in France, Italy and in many smaller European states, and by the rise of UKIP in England. All these trends are also responses to rising economic inequalities, with the blame so often put on new poorer arrivals rather than on those who already take so much of the cake.

The message of both recent trends – the progressivism that appears in so many new forms, and the alarming populism of the right – is that many people in many countries no longer want to accept things as they are. The change that is needed is not just the message of those who would like a kinder politics. Government can make us happier.[225] But only we can create the government that will do that. And if we make the wrong choices, the implications are far-reaching.

When people look back on their lives, they often wish they had done things differently. They wish they had not had to amass such debts, especially in paying for education. They wish one particular relationship had not ended, or that they had been with someone else. They wish they had become a parent. They wish they had said goodbye to their loved ones properly before they died. And they wish that they had not had to worry so much through so much of their life about so many issues that they later realized were quite trivial.[226]

You have just finished reading a book with a list of concrete problems that need solving, ones that really matter to most people in the UK; a book that contains some initial suggestions as to how we might begin to start solving those problems. You need not be young to avoid regret, but if you are young you have more time and, perhaps, a greater incentive. If a better politics were in the direct and obvious interest of the old, wealthy and powerful, it would already exist.

Afterword

This book is based on a few ideas that began with the findings of one academic paper published a decade ago, using data from a decade before that. Those findings are being extrapolated forwards, and I have thrown in many ideas that are buzzing around academia, in books and articles, and reported in newspapers, magazines and elsewhere on the Internet. In all cases I try to give the most accessible source – one that is not hidden behind a paywall – in the endnotes below. Most are not polished ideas and will need rethinking before coming to fruition. Inevitably, some will turn out to be stupid. What is certain is that there is no shortage of ideas and choices.[227]

But before we adopt any ideas, we can all benefit from stepping back and asking what matters most – and why we appear to have forgotten to do this more in the countries, like the UK and the US, that are the most unequal. Then, and only then, can we ask what we should do about it. We know we need a better politics for a happier and healthier future. And we know that no one else will make that politics but us.

Appendix

This appendix provides more information on the ways in which the responses to the open-ended British Household Panel Survey (BHPS) question asking people to state in their own words 'what has happened to you (or your family) which has stood out as important' were coded in the BHPS.

Answers were recorded verbatim, but verbatim responses were not made available for public release because of confidentiality concerns. However, the following numeric codes were developed to capture the full range of events.

Health: 01 ill health/concern about health; 02 hospitalization/operation; 03 accident (involving injury); 04 health tests (positive and negative); 05 loss of mobility/house-bound; 06 recovery/continuing good health; 09 health (not elsewhere classified (NEC)).

Caring: 10 caring responsibilities – not childcare (who is cared for?*); 11 babysitting (who is the sitter?*).

Education: 12 starting/in school; 13 leaving school; 14 starting/in further education (including sixth form); 15 leaving further education; 16 studying for/passing educational/vocational qualifications/acquiring skills/training (NEC); 17 travel related to study; 19 education (NEC).

Employment: 20 change of job (including hours, status)/starting own business; 21 planned/possible change of job; 22 getting job (following economic inactivity); 23 work-related training (including apprenticeship/heavy goods vehicle licence/work experience); 24 redundancy/unemployment (threat of or actual); 25 retirement; 26 travel related to work (who travels?*); 27 work-related problems; 29 jobs/careers (NEC).

Leisure/political: 30 vacation/travel (NEC); 31 leisure activities; 32 learning to drive/passing test (not heavy goods vehicle); 33 political participation/voluntary work (including committee work); 34 reference to national/world events (who is concerned by event?*).

Non-familial relationships: 35 began friendship (including girl/boyfriend); 36 end friendship (including girl/boyfriend); 37 spending time with/visiting friends (coded as holiday as appropriate); 38 problems with neighbours (who has the problem?*); 39 non-family relationship (NEC).

Family events: 40 pregnancy/birth (identity of parent?*); 41 cohabitation; 42 engagements/weddings; 43 separation/divorce/end of cohabitation; 44 leaving parental home; 45 death (who died?*); 46 wedding anniversaries; 47 birthday celebrations; 48 becoming godparent; 50 spending time/visits with relatives (not within household); 51 day-to-day family life; 52 family problems (person causing problems?*); 53 domestic incident (e.g. fire/burst pipes, etc.); 54 pets/animals (pet coded); 59 family event/family reference (NEC).

Financial matters: 60 money problems/drop in income/debt; 61 forced move (repossession/eviction) (move into residential home not included); 62 improved financial situation; 63 received money (inheritance/compensation/pools); 69 financial other (NEC).

Consumption: 70 bought/buying vehicle (car, caravan, etc.); 71 bought/buying/building house; 72 household repairs/improvements/appliances; 73 won prize (not cash)/award; 74 received present (from whom?*); 79 other purchases (NEC).

Residential move: 80 moved in past year; 81 future intention to move; 82 move into residential home (nursing/retirement, etc.); 83 move into respondent's household (who is moving in?*).

Crime: 90 victim of crime (burglary, etc.); 91 committed crime/in trouble with police.

Religion: 92 joined/changed religion; 93 other religious reference (not confirmation/baptism of children).

Other: 94 plan not fulfilled/something that didn't happen (e.g. didn't have a holiday); 95 civil court action/battles with bureaucracy; 96 other occurrence (NEC) given low priority; 97 nothing happened.

---

* People's answers to the BHPS event question included not only events that happened to them personally but also events that happened to other family members or friends. Each event has, therefore, been assigned a subject code as follows: 00 not mentioned; 01 we/household; 02 self (explicit or inferred or no pronoun); 03 spouse/partner; 04 daughter(s); 05 son(s); 06 child(ren) (NEC); 07 son-/daughter-in-law; 08 mother; 09 father; 10 parents (both or not specified); 11 parent(s)-in-law; 12 siblings (sister/brother); 13 sister-in-law/brother-in-law; 14 grandparent(s); 15 grandchild(ren); 16 other family members/family members unspecified; 17 friend/colleague.

Endnotes

1. A century ago geographers were more concerned with war than happiness. The geographical theory 'Who rules East Europe commands the Heartland; who rules the Heartland commands the World-Island; who rules the World-Island commands the world' advocated war and almost brought the world to the brink of a nuclear Third World War: http://bit.ly/1uYytef.

2. A. Marr. 2015 (2nd edn). *Head of State*, p. 15. London: Fourth Estate.

3. D. Massey. 2015. Why the Corbyn leadership is still the best hope for Labour. In *Soundings 61 – Catch the Tide*, editorial. London: Lawrence & Wishart. (See http://bit.ly/23SwkFR.)

4. See E. Weiner. 2009. *The Geography of Bliss*. New York: Twelve. R. Wilkinson and K. Pickett. 2010. *The Spirit Level: Why Equality Is Better for Everyone*. London: Penguin. M. J. Sandel. 2013. *What Money Can't Buy: The Moral Limits of Markets*. New York: Farrar, Straus and Giroux. E. Skidelsky and R. Skidelsky. 2013. *How Much is Enough? Money and the Good Life*. London: Penguin.

5. This writer is a geographer, so this is a journey through happiness that is more wide ranging than an economics lesson. See D. Ballas and D. Dorling. 2013. The geography of happiness. In *Oxford Handbook of Happiness* edited by S. A. David, I. Boniwell and A. Conley Ayers, chapter 36, pp. 465–481. Oxford University Press. (See http://bit.ly/1KlMmBF.)

6. M. Hiltzik (quoting Radcliff). 2013. How much are we willing to pay for the pursuit of happiness? *Los Angeles Times*, 3 November (http://lat.ms/1Klm2aQ).

7. The reason he is correct is explained in A. Barford, K. Pickett and D. Dorling. 2010. Re-evaluating self-evaluation: a commentary

on Jen, Jones, and Johnston (68:4, 2009). *Social Science & Medicine* 70:496–497. (See http://bit.ly/1Q7zWdc.)

8. D. Ballas, D. Dorling, T. Nakaya, H. Tunstall and K. Hanaoka. 2014. Income inequalities in Japan and the UK: a comparative study of two island economies. *Journal of Social Policy and Society* 13(1):103–117. (See http://bit.ly/20C1dvU.)

9. A. J. Oswald. 1997. Happiness and economic performance. Working Paper (subsequently published in *The Economic Journal*). (See http://bit.ly/1JTJBHH.)

10. A. Pettifor. 2006. *The Coming First World Debt Crisis*. London: Palgrave Schol.

11. A. Nesvetailova. 2007. *Fragile Finance: Debt, Speculation and Crisis in the Age of Global Credit*. London: Palgrave Macmillan.

12. A. Stutzer and B. S. Frey. 2012. Recent developments in the economics of happiness: a selective overview. IZA Discussion Paper 7078, p. 12 (http://ftp.iza.org/dp7078.pdf).

13. J. F. Helliwell. 2014. Social norms, happiness, and the environment: closing the circle. *Sustainability: Science, Practice, & Policy* 10(1):1–7. (See http://bit.ly/1nOzMRl.)

14. G. O'Donnell and J. A. Oswald. 2015. National well-being policy and a weighted approach to human feelings. *Journal of Ecological Economics*, forthcoming. (Preprint available at http://bit.ly/1PDe4fu.)

15. United Nations. 2012. Resolution adopted by the General Assembly on 28 June 2012, 66/281, International Day of Happiness (http://bit.ly/1nOzOIO).

16. M. Fleurbaey and H. Schwandt. 2015. Do people seek to maximize their subjective well-being? CEP Discussion Paper 1391, LSE (http://bit.ly/1JTyaQi).

17. Some 35,965 people answered the question in total. Some did so each year. Not everyone completed the survey every year. Just under 10,000 people were interviewed each year. See D. Ballas and D. Dorling. 2007. Measuring the impact of major life events upon happiness. *International Journal of Epidemiology* 36(6):1244–1252. (See http://bit.ly/2036hqU.)

18. Staff Reporter. 2009. Adults forget three things a day, research finds. *The Telegraph*, 23 July (http://bit.ly/1SiMOBJ).

19. Terrorism is not an event that features as one that people report as having affected their lives, because it remains so rare. But if a question is asked about terrorism, for instance in the 2004 presidential election in the United States, then that issue can feature as 'among the most important issues determining their vote choice'. I. H. Indridason. 2008. Does terrorism influence domestic politics? Coalition formation and terrorist incidents. *Journal of Peace Research* 45:241–259 (see p. 245).

20. D. Dorling. 2015 (2nd edn). *Injustice: Why Social Inequality Still Persists*. Bristol: Policy Press. (See figure 21 from this book, which is available at http://bit.ly/1Q7A24t.)

21. R. Mitchell and F. Popham. 2008. Effect of exposure to natural environment on health inequalities: an observational population study. *Lancet* 372(9650):1655–1660. (See http://bit.ly/1OOHpA8.)

22. Geographers traditionally worry about such things, including this one and a colleague recently: D. Dorling and C. Lee. 2016. *Geography*. London: Profile.

23. BBC. 2010. Plan to measure happiness 'not woolly' – Cameron. *BBC UK Politics*, 25 November (http://bbc.in/1Saplix).

24. ONS. 2015. Measuring national well-being, domains and measures – September 2015. Report, ONS (http://bit.ly/1OOHtQe).

25. A. Bryson, J. Forth and L. Stokes. 2015. Happier workers can lead to higher profits. LSE British Politics and Policy blog, 6 August (http://bit.ly/23sD5hz).

26. D. Adams and M. Carwardine. 2009. *Last Chance to See*. London: Arrow.

27. He was trained in Greece where, as in many countries other than the UK and US, economists are also given a wider understanding of the history of economics. For that wider view see H.-J. Chang. 2014. *Economics: The User's Guide: A Pelican Introduction*. London: Pelican.

28. Note that we could have obscured the results even more. We didn't use an 'ordered-probit model', which some economists might

have preferred, and we may have given too colloquial a description of what the constant and coefficients might mean. We also don't explain that the reference category is 'all other combinations of subject and type of event', but we didn't need to. The paper was obscure enough already. However, if you want to know more about these issues, see A. J. Oswald. 2007. Human well-being and causality in social epidemiology. *International Journal of Epidemiology* 36(6):1253–1254 (http://bit.ly/1OOHxPT).

29. A. H. Maslow. 1943. A theory of human motivation. *Psychological Review* 50(4):370–396. (See http://bit.ly/Os2Fkt.)

30. D. Dorling. 2013 (2nd edn). *The Population of the UK*. London: Sage. (See http://bit.ly/1LaE9LH.)

31. M. Blastland and D. Spiegelhalter. 2014. *The Norm Chronicles: Stories and Numbers about Danger*. London: Profile.

32. D. Spiegelhalter. 2015. *Sex by Numbers: What Statistics Can Tell Us about Sexual Behaviour*. London: Profile.

33. If you can't wait for later, then for insights into why people in some cultures are more likely to think they are better than average and having a better time than average, see http://bit.ly/1OOHyn5.

34. M. Shaw, R. Mitchell and D. Dorling. 2000. Time for a smoke: one cigarette is equivalent to 11 minutes of life expectancy. *British Medical Journal* 320:53. (See http://bit.ly/1KlMtgC.)

35. L. Donnelly. 2015. Alarm over sudden drop in female life expectancy. *The Telegraph*, 6 April (http://bit.ly/1IFceTd).

36. Conflict of interest note: the author of this book is a member of the Public Health England (PHE) 2015/2016 Mortality Surveillance Steering Group.

37. D. Dorling. 2014. Why are the old dying before their time? How austerity has affected mortality rates. *New Statesman*, 7 February. (See http://bit.ly/1P0JVTR.)

38. A. Grice. 2014. Women bear 85% of burden after Coalition's tax and benefit tweaks. *The Independent*, 4 December (http://ind.pn/1nxth5x).

39. E. J. Emanuel and L. L. Emanuel. 1998. The promise of a good death. *Lancet* 351(Supplement 2):SII21–29 (http://bit.ly/1OYkxvI).

40. J. Lyons and A. Lines. 2013. Margaret Thatcher dead: she spent final weeks with devoted friends at bedside but not her own children. *The Mirror*, 25 September (http://bit.ly/1Ka8Ntg).

41. I. Wolfe. 2014. Why the UK has a high child death rate. *BBC News*, 3 May (http://bbc.in/1kElUTo).

42. D. Foster. 2015. Can family support reduce Northern Ireland's high infant death rates? *The Guardian*, 25 March (http://bit.ly/1EFNfvz).

43. Around half of the 28% is taken just by the best-off 1% in the UK. The UK also has the highest Gini coefficient of income inequality in Europe (0.351): OECD. 2015. In it together – why less inequality benefits all. Report, OECD. (See http://bit.ly/1AmZloV and particularly chapter 1, Table 1.A1.1: 'Key indicators on the distribution of household disposable income and poverty, 2007, 2011 and 2013 or most recent' (http://bit.ly/1SYWYI6).)

44. A. Offer. 2006. The *Challenge of Affluence: Self-Control and Well-Being in the United States and Britain Since 1950*. Oxford University Press.

45. P. Tambe, H. M. Sammons and I. Choonara. 2015. Why do young children die in the UK? A comparison with Sweden. *Archives of Disease in Childhood*, 13 August, doi:10.1136/archdischild-2014-308059 (http://bit.ly/1JE4Pt2).

46. Pedestrian Safety. 2015. European comparisons of child pedestrian safety: WHO data on deaths in 2010–2012 per 100,000 children (http://bit.ly/1Tnak1g).

47. The Equality Trust. 2015. *Mental health: people in more equal societies are far less likely to experience mental illness*. Report, Equality Trust (http://bit.ly/1LaEvSv).

48. This is partly because gun crime includes the malicious use of air rifles: D. Dorling. 2011. Unique Britain. Open Democracy website article, 15 May (http://bit.ly/1SJvFm4).

49. B. McPartland. 2013. Why France has such a high rate of suicides. *The Local* (Paris correspondent), 10 September (http://bit.ly/1ZSiCOH).

50. Strictly speaking these proportions are for England and Wales, but the UK will be similar, possibly slightly higher in more recent years over that larger geographical extent. See ONS. 2013. What are the top causes of death by age and gender? Statistical Release, 22 October (http://bit.ly/1Gqt1wo).

51. Staff Reporter. 2010. The U-bend of life: why, beyond middle age, people get happier as they get older. *The Economist*, 16 December (http://econ.st/1t3wD1o). Note that this is a global average: it varies by country and far more by individual, although being 48 as I write, it is comforting to think that the most probable way from here on through is up.

52. EMCDDA. 2011. Annual report 2011. The state of the drugs problem in Europe: drug-related infectious diseases and drug-related deaths. European Monitoring Centre for Drugs and Drug Addition, 15 November (http://bit.ly/1VqCXsZ).

53. ONS. 2015. Deaths related to drug poisoning in England and Wales, 2014 registrations. Statistical Bulletin, 3 September (http://bit.ly/1PACm3i).

54. DoH. 2015. Department of Health spokeswoman quoted in 'Drug deaths in England and Wales reach record levels'. *BBC News*, 3 September (http://bbc.in/1PJRLTs).

55. A. Allegretti. 2015. David Cameron slams his own cuts in bitterly ironic letter to Oxford Council. *Huffington Post*, 11 November (http://huff.to/1NtoZOO).

56. J. Whitelegg and G. Haq. 2006. Vision zero: adopting a target of zero for road traffic fatalities and serious injuries. Stockholm Environment Institute (http://bit.ly/1I81tdG).

57. D. C. Richard. 2010. Relationship between speed, risk and fatal injury: pedestrians and car occupants. Report, Department for Transport, p. 14 (http://bit.ly/1NzTvZG).

58. J. Whitelegg. 2015. What would Vision Zero Britain look like? Vision Zero London (http://bit.ly/1RN1WbK).

59. D. Dorling. 2015. Creating a more equal society will require understanding and generosity, hope, perseverance, but above all

kindness. Democratic Audit blog, LSE, 18 December (http://bit.ly/1U9lm75).

60. I am a patron of the charity RoadPeace, so I am not a neutral bystander on road deaths: http://www.roadpeace.org/.

61. D. Campbell. 2015. NHS workplace stress could push 80% of senior doctors to early retirement. *The Guardian*, 10 September (http://bit.ly/1F0OfkB).

62. A. Gregory. 2015. Britain's healthcare lagging behind the rest of the world. *The Mirror*, 4 November (http://bit.ly/1VqD87H).

63. M. Silver. 2015. The increasing death toll due to the loss of benefits. *Vox Political*, 13 September (http://bit.ly/1OYl94J).

64. R. Barr, D. Taylor-Robinson, D. Stuckler, R. Loopstra, A. Reeves and M. Whitehead. 2015. 'First, do no harm': are disability assessments associated with adverse trends in mental health? A longitudinal ecological study. *Journal of Epidemiology Community Health*, doi:10.1136/jech-2015-206209.

65. J. Kirby. 2015. 'Fit to work' policy linked to suicides. *Western Daily Press*, 16 November (http://bit.ly/1UpH4FF).

66. Dr Lynne Friedli, who co-authored the paper making this assessment (reference 67 below) had a few years earlier, in 2009, authored the World Health Organisation report on mental health, resilience and inequality. (See http://bit.ly/1NzTBAF.)

67. L. Friedli and R. Stearn. 2015. Positive affect as coercive strategy: conditionality, activation and the role of psychology in UK government workfare programmes. *Critical Medical Humanities* 41:40–47 (reference 86: doi:10.1136/medhum-2014-010622) (http://bit.ly/1MB9KrD).

68. OECD. 2015. Focus on health spending: OECD health statistics 2015. Report, OECD. (Data extracted in December: http://bit.ly/1qtVKpJ.)

69. A colleague who grew up in Eastern Europe told me recently that it was shocking to see television documentaries on how the administration 'thinks' and 'works' here in Britain. Our administration is designed in a way to have regulations, rules and norms

that 'distance' (in a very polite manner) the administrator from the person in his/her care, so they can send them away at the end of a meeting/consultation and then turn to the camera and ask the reporter: 'Have you seen how unreasonably they behaved?' One case my colleague had in mind was of a woman with three children who all ended up on the streets and were not helped in any way for months because they weren't able to produce some stupid piece of paper that, according to the rulebook, was requested of them if they wanted to be housed. And then as the film went on it became clearer and clearer that the council had no resources to house these families, so they quickly invented a set of new criteria and sorted people based on these formal criteria. They could then tell them (and the television documentary viewer) that it was people's fault they were not helped because they did not want to 'cooperate'. The aim of the documentary was to try to show how 'unreasonable' and 'uncivilized' these poor people were.

70. M. Adler. 2015. Benefit sanctions and the rule of law. Paper presented at the Annual Conference of the Law Society of Scotland, Edinburgh International Conference Centre, 2 October. (See http://bit.ly/1Tx6zGz.)

71. The Fawcett Society. 2015. Where's the benefit? An independent inquiry into women and Jobseeker's Allowance. Report, Fawcett Society, 6 February (http://bit.ly/1lRbSD6).

72. John retired in April 2014, but he continues to work in health as an honorary professor of public health (http://bit.ly/1pylm1r).

73. J. Middleton. 2015. Why is there acute hunger in the UK and what is to be done about it? British Medical Journal blog, 19 November (http://bit.ly/20s6JAY).

74. N. Stotesbury and D. Dorling. 2015. Understanding income inequality and its implications: why better statistics are needed. Statistics Views, 21 October. (See http://bit.ly/20BOEkd.)

75. J. Warner. 2015. Paying all UK citizens £155 a week may be an idea whose time has come. The Telegraph, 8 December (http://bit.ly/1R5pbgN).

76. R. Ramesh. 2012. Two-child benefits policy targets the strivers in low-paid jobs. *The Guardian*, 25 October (http://bit.ly/1PDfPt9).

77. A. Chakelian. 2015. Budget 2015: what welfare changes did George Osborne announce, and what do they mean? *New Statesman*, 8 July (http://bit.ly/1QrCh5t).

78. D. Dorling. 2015 (2nd edn). *All that Is Solid: How the Great Housing Disaster Defines Our Times, and What We Can Do About It*. London: Allen Lane. (See http://bit.ly/1P0K6i5.)

79. D. Dorling and B. Thomas. 2016 (forthcoming). *People and Places: A Twenty-First Century Census Atlas*. Bristol: Policy Press.

80. D. Ballas, D. Dorling and B. D. Hennig. 2014. *The Social Atlas of Europe*, p.41. Bristol: Policy Press (the updated version of this atlas detailing the fall in numbers will be published at the end of 2016).

81. R. Sanghani. 2015. Maternity discrimination forcing thousands of new UK mums out of work. *The Telegraph*, 24 July (http://bit.ly/1OBtM6j).

82. D. Dorling. 2015. Income inequality in the UK: comparisons with five large Western European countries and the USA. *Applied Geography* 61:24–34. (See http://bit.ly/1KlMEbv.)

83. J. Hall. 2012. Average first-time buyer is now 35. *The Telegraph*, 11 September (http://bit.ly/1kRXBDn).

84. Figure 1 is a simplification of a more complicated diagram in which cells are coloured darkest in the figure if more than 70% of people in that year and of that age owned or had a mortgage. Cells are coloured lightest if less than 50% did. It appears that home-ownership is becoming a thing of the past. The original diagram is shown here: D. Dorling. 2015. Only one lucky generation ever struck housing gold. *The Telegraph*, 27 April (http://bit.ly/1QFcjvS).

85. D. Dorling. 2015. Data on income inequality in Germany, France, Italy, Spain, the UK, and comparisons to other affluent nations. *Data in Brief* 5:458–460. (See http://bit.ly/1okse95.)

86. S. Ashton, M. Francis and M. Jarvie. 2015. Too poor to pay: the impact of the second year of localized council tax support in London. Report, Child Poverty Action Group/Zacchaeus 2000 Trust, July (http://bit.ly/1ha4qRO).

87. New Policy Institute. 2015. London's poverty profile 2015. Report, Trust for London (http://bit.ly/1PFZTnQ).

88. K. Barker. 2014. *Housing: Where's the Plan?* London Publishing Partnership (http://bit.ly/1PACHTC).

89. P. Moskowitz. 2015. San Francisco's deepening rent crisis pushes out vulnerable teachers. *The Guardian*, 10 September (http://bit.ly/1gcFxUt).

90. S. J. Smith. 2014. Japan shows the way to affordable megacities. *Next City*, 22 January (http://bit.ly/1KEAPbh).

91. M. Fransham. 2015. Housing: rising prices, low sales, deteriorating affordability. Chart of the Month, Oxford City Council, 24 September (http://bit.ly/1QmyOT1).

92. S. Butler. 2015. Pace of rent rises quickens as average UK rent reaches £937 a month. *The Guardian*, 24 August (http://bit.ly/1NOSDTn).

93. H. Osborne. 2015. London house prices most overvalued in the world, says UBS. *The Guardian*, 29 October (http://bit.ly/1M3u2Mb).

94. M. Taylor. 2015. 'Vast social cleansing' pushes tens of thousands of families out of London. *The Guardian*, 28 August (http://bit.ly/1PWQgiN).

95. T. Slater. 2015. Why we need rent controls. Living Rent Campaign blog, 10 September (http://bit.ly/1RQSbtl).

96. ONS. 2015. Relationship between wealth, income and personal well-being, July 2011 to June 2012. Report, Office for National Statistics (http://bit.ly/1lRcBEg).

97. P. Collinson. 2015. One in 65 UK adults now a millionaire. *The Guardian*, 27 August (http://bit.ly/1MPz92u).

98. T. Carey. 2015. Why being an accidental millionaire doesn't make you feel rich: one in 65 people may now be millionaires, but as Tanith Carey has discovered, the lifestyle's not what it used to be... *The Telegraph*, 27 August (http://bit.ly/1SJwcof).

99. J. Treanor. 2015. Half of world's wealth now in hands of 1% of population. *The Guardian*, 13 October (http://bit.ly/1MoQopb).

100. Staff Reporter. 2015. If the world introduces a 'Piketty tax': squeezing the rich. *The Economist*, 30 July (print edition; online at http://bit.ly/1IPh3Mu).

101. C. Collins and J. Hoxie. 2015. *Billionaire Bonanza: The Forbes 400 and the Rest of Us*. Washington, DC: Institute for Policy Studies (http://bit.ly/1O3EKoV).

102. E. N. Wolff. 2012. The asset price meltdown and the wealth of the middle class. Occasional Paper, New York University, table 4, p. 60 (http://bit.ly/204aL5K).

103. K. Allen. 2015. Evictions soar in England and Wales as benefit cuts bite. *Financial Times*, 13 August (http://on.ft.com/1SaqZWK).

104. See Becky Tunstall's graph (figure 13) at http://bit.ly/1QQbbVU.

105. N. Falk. 2014. Funding housing and local growth: how a British investment bank can help. Report, Smith Institute, p. 13 (http://bit.ly/1RN2qik).

106. Simon calls me a housing economist when he agrees with me and a geographer when he does not, which I am not sure is a compliment. See S. Jenkins. 2015. Forget new homes, we aren't making use of what we already have. *Evening Standard*, 6 October (http://bit.ly/1LyqwLn).

107. H. Haber. 2015. Regulation as social policy: home evictions and repossessions in the UK and Sweden. *Public Administration* 93:806–821.

108. U. Huws. 2015. The road from Damascus. Blog post, 25 September (http://bit.ly/1VqE4c7).

109. D. Dorling. 2015 (2nd edn). *Injustice: Why Social Inequality Still Persists*. Bristol: Policy Press. (See http://bit.ly/TF2Z1u.)

110. G. Wood. 2011. Secret fears of the super-rich. *The Atlantic*, April (http://theatln.tc/1BXTHO2).

111. I. Graham. 2015. Countries compared by people: divorce rate. International Statistics, Nation Master (http://bit.ly/1tf9Jlj; accessed October).

112. K. Williams, V. Papadopoulou and N. Booth. 2012. Prisoners' childhood and family backgrounds: results from the Surveying

Prisoner Crime Reduction (SPCR) longitudinal cohort study of prisoners. Ministry of Justice Research Series 4/12 (http://bit.ly/1wKXPm9).

113. R. Garside. 2015. Better an ideologue than a barbarian: Michael Gove is a refreshing change from his predecessor as Justice Secretary, but he should leave out the God-talk. Centre for Crime and Justice Studies blog post, 9 October (http://bit.ly/1KaagQr).

114. Department for Education and Skills. 2003. Every child matters. Stationery Office (most recently quoted in 2015: http://bit.ly/1QrCHbR).

115. People, including children, do tend to have more punitive and vindictive attitudes in more unequal societies. This can result in odd and highly publicized research findings with any international studies that include the US in their sample, such as J. Decety, J. M. Cowell, K. Lee, R. Mahasneh, S. Malcolm-Smith, B. Selcuk and X. Zhou. 2015. The negative association between religiousness and children's altruism across the world. *Current Biology* 25(22):2951–2955 (http://bit.ly/1TnbF8n).

116. 'Legislative and policy changes have contributed to more stringent outcomes, making sentence lengths longer for certain offences and increasing the likelihood of imprisonment for breach of a non-custodial sentence or failure to comply with licence conditions.' Ministry of Justice. 2013. Story of the prison population: 1993–2012, England and Wales, prison and probation statistics. Report, Ministry of Justice, p. 21 (http://bit.ly/20s73zU).

117. Home Office. 2015. Hate crimes, England and Wales 2014 to 2015. Government Statistical Service, 13 October (http://bit.ly/1MwzGHp).

118. On our fear of the poor see J. Unwin. 2013. *Why Fight Poverty?* London Publishing Partnership (http://bit.ly/18EWxsT).

119. J. Bingham. 2015. Alan Yentob under fire for alarmist Kids Company claims. *The Telegraph*, 15 October (http://bit.ly/1G8fc6O).

120. D. Dorling and C. Lee. 2014. Inequality constitutes a particular place. In *Riot, Unrest and Protest on the Global Stage*, edited by D. Pritchard and F. Pakes, chapter 7, pp. 115–131. Basingstoke: Palgrave Macmillan. (See http://bit.ly/1KSBPJo.)

121. R. Garside. 2015. Prison building 'short-sighted and contradictory'. Report, Centre for Crime and Justice Studies, 9 November (http://bit.ly/1nOB9Q1).

122. R. Roberts. 2015. Criminal justice 'transformation': a wolf in sheep's clothing? Report, Centre for Crime and Justice Studies, 15 October (http://bit.ly/1KAFP67).

123. Dorling (2015): see note 59.

124. M. Orton. 2015. Something's not right: insecurity and an anxious nation. Report, Compass (http://bit.ly/1UpHTOK).

125. Reducing our addiction to accountancy would be only a small step towards becoming less anxious, but it could help. At any one time we have 165,000 students registered for training to become professional accountants, and a further 100,000 students studying for a degree in accountancy – this is more than in medicine and many other caring and healing subjects combined. It may appear strange to jump from anxiety to accountancy, but it is an anxious country that feels the need to employ so many people to check the books over and over again.

126. P. Sikka. 2009. A nation of accountants. *The Guardian*, 13 June (http://bit.ly/1KaasPK).

127. Just after the line: 'They must feel the thrill of totting up a balanced book, a thousand ciphers neatly in a row'. M. Poppins. 1964. *A British Bank (The Life I Lead)*. Burbank, CA: Disney (http://bit.ly/1KAFQXJ). (The actual songwriters were R. M. Sherman and R. B. Sherman.)

128. D. Madland. 2015. *Hollowed Out: Why the Economy Doesn't Work without a Strong Middle Class*, p. 47. Oakland, CA: University of California Press.

129. R. P. Formisano. 2015. *Plutocracy in America*. Baltimore, MD: John Hopkins University Press.

130. Dorling and Thomas (2016): see note 79.

131. D. Ballas, D. Dorling and B. D. Hennig. 2016. *The Human Atlas of Europe: A Continent United in Diversity*. Bristol: Policy Press (forthcoming).

132. D. Dorling and C. Lee. 2016. *Geography*. London: Profile (forthcoming).

133. Dorling (2015): see note 109.

134. P. Mason. 2015. The end of capitalism has begun. *The Guardian*, 17 July (http://bit.ly/1GpQTKp).

135. From *In Memoriam A. H. H.*, canto 27: 'I envy not in any moods' (http://bit.ly/1Q4TjJY). On the evidence, see: D. Dorling and M. Shaw. 2000. Life chances and lifestyles. In *The Changing Geography of the UK*, edited by V. Gardiner and H. Matthews, chapter 12, pp. 230–260. London: Routledge (http://bit.ly/1KlMQYs).

136. International Labour Organisation. 2015. Where is the unemployment rate the highest. Global Employment Trends, provisional data for 2015 (http://bit.ly/1wpVeMv).

137. M. Scott Cato. 2008. *Green Economics: An Introduction to Theory, Policy and Practice*. London: Routledge.

138. M. Mazzucato. 2015. *The Entrepreneurial State: Debunking Public vs. Private Sector Myths*. New York: Public Affairs.

139. K. Raworth. 2012. A safe and just space for humanity. Oxfam Discussion Paper, February (http://bit.ly/204beFb).

140. D. Dorling. 2013. Fairness and the changing fortunes of people in Britain. *Journal of the Royal Statistical Society* A176(1):97–128 (http://bit.ly/1Q7B1l8).

141. D. Dorling. 2015 (2nd edn). *Inequality and the 1%*. London: Verso. (See http://bit.ly/1KuXCtx.)

142. J. Hutchinson and T. Thornhill. 2015. Around 1,700 private jets flying in to Davos... for World Economic Forum meeting to discuss climate change and global warming. *Daily Mail*, 19 January (http://dailym.ai/1CNbcl2).

143. A. Wooldridge. 2015. The sad, sick life of the business traveller. *The Economist*, 17 August (http://econ.st/1JdF704).

144. Some are referenced in these endnotes, but a quick Internet search will find you many more references to problems in the personal and professional lives of those at the top. The Internet makes it harder to control the media and harder to hide.

145. R. Steiner. 2015. WPP faces shareholder anger as it awards boss Sir Martin Sorrell with £43m pay package. *Daily Mail*, 30 April (http://bit.ly/1QCoKqu).

146. P. Sellers. 2015. Britain now most unequal EU country, says official report. TUC Touchstone blog, 18 May (http://bit.ly/1FtI8Fg).

147. G. Hiscott. 2015. Morrisons may be hiking wages above the living wage but there's a sting in the tail. *The Mirror*, 29 September (http://bit.ly/1OOJAUa).

148. C. Tavris and E. Aronson. 2013 (updated edn). *Mistakes Were Made (but Not by Me): Why We Justify Foolish Beliefs, Bad Decisions and Hurtful Acts*, p. 66. London: Pinter and Martin.

149. NAO. 2015. Short guides to government. National Audit Office, (https://www.nao.org.uk/search/pi_area/short-guides/type/repo rt/). (The reports for the year before are at https://www.nao.org.uk/ Collections/short-guides-to-departments/.)

150. NEF. 2015. Fairness commissions: understanding how local authorities can have an impact on inequality and poverty. Report, New Economics Foundation, p. 19 (http://bit.ly/1E3V195).

151. C. Pleasance. 2014. Sweden introduces a six-hour working day in bid to reduce sick leave, boost efficiency and make staff happier. *Daily Mail*, 9 April (http://dailym.ai/1qpQdow).

152. A. Shaw. 2015. Fancy a six hour work day? *New Zealand Herald*, 8 October (http://bit.ly/1Tnc9vg).

153. S. Kumar. 2015. What the US could learn from Sweden's 6-hour work day. *Fortune Magazine*, 6 October (http://for.tn/1jNHxVA).

154. J. Ostroff. 2015. The Dutch city of Utrecht is doling out free money for a 'basic income' experiment. *Huffington Post*, 7 October (http://huff.to/1PS1XFB).

155. AFP. 2015. Finland to test unconditional basic income for Finns in 2017. EurActiv (Agence France-Presse), 9 December(http://bit. ly/1RB9wWM).

156. Mason (2015): see note 134.

157. P. Mason. 2015. *PostCapitalism: A Guide to Our Future*. London: Allen Lane.

158. M. Allen. 2015. *Hard Labour: Young People Moving into Work in Difficult Times*. London: Radicaled Books (http://bit.ly/1PS21Fc).

159. R. Urie. 2015. Capitalism run amok: hungry kids, falling wages and empty houses. *Counterpunch*, 18 September (http://bit.ly/1LHXm6D).

160. In the US, 'Conservative politics relies on the middle class making a devil's bargain, believing they have more in common with the rich than the poor. It won't be long before that facade crumbles.' From S. McElwee. 2015. Welcome to feudalism, America: how the 1 percent is systematically destroying the middle class. *Salon*, 1 June (http://bit.ly/1UpIjEH).

161. CPAG. 2015. Welfare reform and work bill 2015, issue 247, August. Child Poverty Action Group (http://bit.ly/1SJwzza).

162. A. Garnham. 2015. When David Cameron became Tory leader, he wanted to end child poverty. Now he just wants to stop measuring it. *New Statesman*, 7 December (http://bit.ly/20s7nOZ).

163. P. Johnson. 2015. Opening remarks, IFS post-spending review/ autumn statement analysis (26 November). Institute for Fiscal Studies (http://bit.ly/1XtfPdy).

164. C. Beatty and S. Fothergill. 2014. The impact of welfare reform on communities and households in Sheffield. CRESR, Sheffield, 26 November (http://bit.ly/1RN3oMX).

165. FRA. 2014. Violence against women: an EU-wide survey. FRA – European Union Agency for Fundamental Rights, Luxembourg (http://bit.ly/1BSvRbD).

166. S. Narotzky. 1997. *New Directions in Economic Anthropology*, p. 114–157. London: Pluto.

167. Personal communications with Vivienne Hayes, Ila Chandavarkar and Florence Rose Burton. 2015. Women's Resource Centre (http://thewomensresourcecentre.org.uk).

168. Some eleven women's organizations came together in 2015 to create a campaign asking politicians to do something about the gap between men and women. Their details are on a resulting website here: http://bit.ly/1JTJT1c.

169. C. Cohen. 2015. The government is planning to 'drop feminism' from the politics A-level. *The Telegraph*, 19 November (http://bit.ly/1HZiWba).

170. The Fawcett Societ. 2015. Giving with one hand, taking away with two – the 2015 Budget. Report, Fawcett Society, 8 July (http://bit.ly/1MhgmLb).

171. On what is being asked for, see http://fairdealforwomen.com/.

172. D. Foster. 2016. *Lean Out*. London: Repeater Books (http://bit.ly/1NzV21Z).

173. T. Eagleton. 2015. The slow death of the university. *Chronicle of Higher Education*, 6 April (http://bit.ly/1NWu6wR).

174. Including those that suggest it would be good to know if it were better to write 'syllabi' or 'syllabuses'!

175. S. Tomlinson (personal correspondence, but drawing on Department for Education 2015 figures). 2015. Permanent and fixed period exclusions in England: 2013 to 2014. Department for Education, Statistical First Release, 30 July (http://bit.ly/1SbhO8g).

176. S. Scott, M. Knapp, J. Henderson and B. Maughan. 2001. Financial cost of social exclusion: follow up study of antisocial children into adulthood. *British Medical Journal* 323:191–194 (http://bit.ly/1JE77IF).

177. T. Wrigley. 2015. A few anomalies? No, baseline is flawed from start to finish. Reclaim Schools blog, 20 November (http://bit.ly/1NkxR28).

178. The static is 4.4 times = $(25/7)/(75/93)$. However, note that it may be higher given extra private tutoring, pre-school fees and university attendance of this small group of students. The more recent figures can be found on p. 93 of EU. 2012. Key data on education in Europe 2012. Education, Audio-visual and Culture Executive Agency, Brussels (http://bit.ly/1WNrK7e).

179. Stotesbury and Dorling (2015): see note 74.

180. K. Pickett and K. Vanderbloemen. 2015. Mind the gap: tackling social and educational inequality. Cambridge Primary Review Trust Report 4 (http://bit.ly/1PDhK0N).

181. Stotesbury and Dorling (2015): see note 74.

182. See N. Duffell. 2014. *Wounded Leaders: British Elitism and the Entitlement Illusion – A Psychohistory*. Lone Arrow Press. (Also see many blog and other pieces on the web, including http://bit.ly/1nxuKZu.)

183. S. Tomlinson. 2015. Special education and minority ethnic young people in England: continuing issues. Discourse: Studies in the Cultural Politics of Education, p. 11 (http://bit.ly/1ZSkzdM) (summarizing the work of Roger Slee).

184. A. McSmith. 2015. How thousands fail the poshness test. *Lifestyle Magazine*, 15 June (http://bit.ly/1PDhPkU; sourced from *The Independent*).

185. L. Ashley, J. Duberley, H. Sommerlad and D. Scholarious. 2015. A qualitative evaluation of non-educational barriers to the elite professions. Report, Social Mobility and Child Poverty Commission, London, June, final page of main report (http://bit.ly/1TnbgSD).

186. As reported by the Sutton Trust in a series of widely publicized studies (www.suttontrust.com).

187. Team GB excels especially, but not exclusively, in 'the sitting down sports' of riding and rowing.

188. M. Wayne and D. O'Neill. 2013. The gentrification of the left. *New Left Project*, 19 August (http://bit.ly/1lReEs2).

189. S. Price. 2014. How my research into pop's posh takeover was hijacked. *The Observer*, 23 February (http://bit.ly/1jq24dl).

190. E. Gosden. 2015. The arts really are dominated by the middle classes, study shows. *The Telegraph*, 23 November (http://bit.ly/1kPDmcK).

191. O. Jones. 2013. *Chavs: The Demonization of the Working Class*. London: Verso.

192. G. Cory and B. Davies. 2015. Following the tax credit row, the welfare axe could fall on renters and disabled claimants. *New Statesman*, 19 November (http://bit.ly/1LovkMK).

193. R. Brown. 2013. We build character as well. *Oxford Times*, 12 September (http://bit.ly/1nOBMcf).

194. HEFCE. 2015. Differences in degree outcomes: the effect of subject and student characteristics. Report, Higher Education Funding Council for England (http://bit.ly/1UXhWEZ).

195. A. McKnight. 2015. Downward mobility, opportunity hoarding and the 'glass floor'. Research Report, Social Mobility and Child Poverty Commission, June (http://bit.ly/1KrinEl).

196. See the website of the Equality Trust: www.equalitytrust.org.uk/.

197. M. Savage, N. Cunningham, F. Devine, S. Friedman, D. Laurison, L. McKenzie, A. Miles, H. Snee and P. Wakeling. 2015. *Social Class in the 21st Century*. London: Pelican.

198. N. Hillman. 2015. Keeping up with the Germans? A comparison of student funding, internationalisation and research in UK and German universities. Higher Education Policy Institute Report 77, Oxford (http://bit.ly/1PAE84F).

199. S. Coughlan. 2010. Majority of young women in university. *BBC News*, 31 March (http://bbc.in/1QrDiui).

200. R. Brown. 2010. *Higher Education and the Market*, p. 12 of chapter 13. London: Routledge.

201. A. Izaguirre. 2015. A tale of two chancellors: income inequality between admins and adjuncts at CUNY. *Kingsman Paper*, 11 May.

202. A. Josuweit. 2015. Student debt is already a hallmark issue for 2016. *Huffington Post*, 4 November (http://huff.to/1WNrWTQ).

203. Climate change activists like to quote the thirteenth-century Persian theologian and poet Rumi at this point: 'Sit, be still, and listen / because you're drunk / and we're at / the edge of the roof.'

204. T. Macalister. 2015. Second solar firm in two days goes bust, blaming UK government policy. *The Guardian*, 8 October (http://bit.ly/1JUNyox).

205. Editorial. 2015. The *Observer* view on the Tory renewable energy policy. *The Observer*, 11 October (http://bit.ly/1PAEcBe).

206. J. M. Keynes. 1931. *Essays in Persuasion*. London: Macmillan. ('Economic possibilities for our grandchildren' (1930), section II: http://bit.ly/1QQcYdw.)

207. Keynes: 'Economic possibilities for our grandchildren' (see immediately above).

208. See the annual statistics produced in the 'Household Below Average Income' statistical series on children living in families that cannot afford a week's holiday a year, not staying with relatives.

209. Foreword to M. Orton. 2015. Secure and free: 10 foundations for a flourishing nation. Report, Compass, September (http://bit.ly/1JE7ByA).

210. T. Veblen. 1899. *The Theory of the Leisure Class: An Economic Study of Institutions*. New York: Macmillan (http://bit.ly/1G09ADr).

211. D. MacShane. 2015. Are things really as bad as we think? *Tribune*, 9 October (http://bit.ly/1RN3uCl).

212. D. Bloom. 2015. Britain's living wage blackspots revealed: find pay packets in your area with our handy search tool. *The Mirror*, 12 October (http://bit.ly/1KECs8Z).

213. R. Murphy. 2015. *The Joy of Tax*. London: Bantam.

214. R. Gregory. 2011. Germany – Freiburg – Green City. Eco Tipping Points blog, January (http://bit.ly/UbGe64).

215. Orton (2015): see note 209.

216. S. Brittan. 1995. *Capitalism with a Human Face*. Cheltenham: Edward Elgar.

217. R. Scruton. 2014. *How to Be a Conservative*. London: A&C Black.

218. 'We humans are the inconvenient gut-flora of the corporation. They aren't hostile to us. They aren't sympathetic to us. Just as every human carries a hundred times more non-human cells in her gut than she has in the rest of her body, every corporation is made up of many separate living creatures that it relies upon for its survival, but which are fundamentally interchangeable and disposable for its purposes. Just as you view stray gut-flora that attacks you as a pathogen and fight it off with antibiotics, corporations attack their human adversaries with an impersonal viciousness that is all the more terrifying for its lack of any emotional heat.' This quote comes from C. Doctorow. 2015. Skynet ascendant. *Locus Magazine*, July (http://bit.ly/1R8mH1V).

219. OECD. 2015. Focus on health spending: OECD health statistics 2015. Report, OECD, data extracted in December (http://bit.ly/1qtVKpJ).

220. D. Dorling. 2015. 'Kinder politics' is only possible if more of those who'll benefit can vote. *The Independent*, 1 October (http://ind.pn/1R4NyMb).

221. R. Johnston, C. Pattie and D. Rossiter. 2015. Ensuring equal representation in Parliament: who counts? LSE British Policy and Politics blog, 20 July (http://bit.ly/1SJx2lo).

222. A. S. Gerber, G. A. Huber, M. Meredith, D. R. Biggers and D. J. Hendry. 2015. Can incarcerated felons be (re)integrated into the political system? Results from a field experiment. *American Journal of Political Science* 59:912–926 (http://bit.ly/20jvZrd).

223. Sheila Ramsay, Chester Labour Party, personal communication, October 2015.

224. D. Dorling and C. Mullin. 2015. Should parliament move out of London? *The Observer*, 7 March (http://bit.ly/1Ew0f9D).

225. B. Headey, R. Muffels and G. G. Wagner. 2010. Long-running German panel survey shows that personal and economic choices, not just genes, matter for happiness. *Proceedings of the National Academy of Sciences of the USA* 107(42):17922–17926 (http://bit.ly/1KabTh1).

226. R. Gillett. 2015. People weighed in on the most common regrets in life, and some of their answers will make you cry. *Business Insider*, 29 November (http://bit.ly/1okvYYb).

227. It helps to look at a wide range of evidence. As Richard Easterlin so succinctly explained almost twenty years ago: 'it is good to be an economist, it is better to be a social scientist': R. A. Easterlin. 1997. The story of a reluctant economist. *The American Economist*. (Revised draft, January 1997, p. 19, available at http://bit.ly/1SSX8BZ.)

Key papers authored by Danny Dorling

D. Dorling. 2010. All connected? Geographies of race, death, wealth, votes and births. *Geographical Journal* 176(3):186–198 (http://bit.ly/1mnfWLM).

D. Dorling. 2013. Crises and turning points: the turning points of history. *Renewal* 21(4):11–20 (http://bit.ly/1T8hes4).

D. Dorling. 2014. How only some rich countries recently set out to become more unequal. *Sociologia, Problemas e Práticas* 74:9–30 (http://bit.ly/1nXM8a6).

D. Dorling. 2015. The mother of underlying causes – economic ranking and health inequality. *Social Science & Medicine* 128:327–330 (http://bit.ly/1PJUIDw).

PERSPECTIVES

Series editor: Diane Coyle

Jim O'Neill's *The BRIC Road to Growth* (published 2013) calls for an urgent overhaul of global economic governance to reflect the reality of the economic power of the BRIC countries and others, especially Korea. Even though their growth rates will slow compared with recent decades, they are key players in the global economy. Jim argues that while the BRIC countries all have stabilizing adjustments to make, there is much for the developed nations in the West to learn from them.

ISBN: 978-1-907994-13-5

Bridget Rosewell's *Reinventing London* (published 2013) tells the story of a city that has enjoyed an extraordinary period of growth in the past generation, symbolized by the towers of Canary Wharf built on the skeleton of the old docks. Finance was at the heart of this, so how can London's economy be reinvented after the financial crisis? An early decision on airport investment to improve global links is a must, given that the capital's main airport is full to capacity.

ISBN: 978-1-907994-14-2

Andrew Sentance's *Rediscovering Growth: After the Crisis* (published 2013) discusses the difficult economic climate in Europe and the US and predicts that it is set to continue for many years, despite desperate efforts to stimulate growth. The long phase of expansion in Western economies that lasted from the 1980s until 2008 was driven by easy money, cheap imports and confidence – all gone.

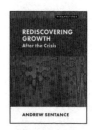

ISBN: 978-1-907994-15-9

Julia Unwin's *Why Fight Poverty?* (published 2013) looks back at the struggle to end poverty and asks if it has been worth it. What would a poverty-free country be like? Julia concludes that we urgently need to resolve poverty, because it is costly, wasteful and risky, but that we can only create a strong, shared understanding of poverty and how to end it when we recognize that 'they' are people like 'us'.

ISBN: 978-1-907994-16-6

David Birch's *Identity Is The New Money* (published 2014) argues that identity is changing profoundly and that money is changing equally profoundly. Because of technological change the two trends are converging so that all that we need for transacting will be our identities captured in the unique record of our online social contacts. Social networks and mobile phones are the key technologies.

ISBN: 978-1-907994-12-8

Kate Barker's *Housing: Where's the Plan?* (published 2014) argues that home ownership is out of reach of a growing number of people. Government finds it easier to introduce short-term policies that are not really effective, meaning that the long-term issues are never really resolved. Reforms are urgently needed. This book dispels some common myths, and provides answers in the form of policy recommendations.

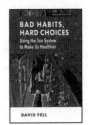

ISBN: 978-1-907994-11-1

David Fell's *Bad Habits, Hard Choices: Using the Tax System to Make Us Healthier* (published 2016) argues that the curious mix of taxes and duties the British face are messy, opaque, out of date – and unfair, with more of your income going to pay these taxes the poorer you are. Drawing on insights from behavioural economics, David concludes that there is a fair, inclusive, adaptable, affordable and resilient way of enabling us to eat healthily and to tackle the obesity crisis.

ISBN: 978-1-907994-50-0

Christian Wolmar's *Are Trams Socialist?* (published spring 2016) argues that it is not too far fetched to say that there has never been a transport policy in the UK – and one is clearly needed. The book suggests elements that such a policy could include.

ISBN: 978-1-907994-56-2

All titles in the **Perspectives** series are available to buy from London Publishing Partnership's website with free UK postage and packing:

http://londonpublishingpartnership.co.uk/perspectives-series/